a fish growing lungs

Published by Burrow Press
PO Box 533709
Orlando, FL 32853
burrowpress.com

Book design: Ryan Rivas
Cover image: Anna_leni

POD Edition, 2021
ISBN: 978-1-941681-14-5
Library of Congress Control Number: 2019948281

a fish growing lungs

alysia li ying sawchyn

essays

BURROW PRESS | ORLANDO, FL

advance praise for...

"...a refreshingly open-ended collection that provides a model of how essay writing can be used for self-exploration."
– PUBLISHERS WEEKLY

"Chilling... bracingly honest... visceral... A potent cautionary tale about the dangers of psychiatric misdiagnoses and the stigma of mental illness." **- KIRKUS REVIEWS**

"...a captivating collection that invites a conversation about how we approach human suffering." **- FOREWORD REVIEWS**

"The essays in *A Fish Growing Lungs* offer an intimate, vulnerable, and entirely spellbinding exploration of addiction, identity, and one writer's struggle to become whole. This debut collection is searingly honest, beautifully written, and Alysia Sawchyn is a fresh new voice."
– DINTY W. MOORE, AUTHOR OF *BETWEEN PANIC & DESIRE*

"*A Fish Growing Lungs* cracks open the necessary conversation about doubt in the ever-changing world of mental health. Here Sawchyn unfurls her life of the misdiagnosed with blunt honesty and unapologetic vulnerability. This new voice in American literature will command your attention, will say what needs to be said, will question and doubt and enlighten, and, in the end, you will be dancing in a glorious light."
- IRA SUKRUNGRUANG, AUTHOR OF *BUDDHA'S DOG & OTHER MEDITATIONS*

"With each sentence of these finely crafted and honed essays, Sawchyn pursues the membrane between lie and truth, illness and degrees of wellness, and the present and the past. A thoughtful precision and honesty allows her to present a deeply satisfying yet open-ended account of living with pain and working to make sense of all we inherit."
- SONYA HUBER, AUTHOR OF *PAIN WOMAN TAKES YOUR KEYS & OTHER ESSAYS FROM A NERVOUS SYSTEM*

... a fish growing lungs

"Sawchyn's omnivorous ponderings are often funny—both ha-ha and strange—conveying a kind of reality where everything, it seems, is misdiagnosed, categorized to fit conditions that require illusions, which *A Fish Growing Lungs* helps us shed."

- PATRICK MADDEN, AUTHOR OF *SUBLIME PHYSICK*

"At once heartfelt and intellectually rigorous, *A Fish Growing Lungs* chronicles a young woman's journey out of the murky waters of self-harm toward the breathable air of health and understanding. Sawchyn is eloquent on the heartbreak of loss. She is equally compelling in portraying a cautious hope for growth and forgiveness."

- KYOKO MORI, AUTHOR OF *YARN: REMEMBERING THE WAY HOME*

"Sawchyn uses all the tools in an essayist's belt to reject the easy binaries we see in many personal narratives: wellness/disorder, injury/recovery, or past/future. *A Fish Growing Lungs* works instead to show how the majority of living occurs in grayer spaces where multiple modes of being are not just possible; they are inevitable."

- ELENA PASSARELLO, AUTHOR OF *ANIMALS STRIKE CURIOUS POSES*

"Beautifully crafted and often inventive essays with the wise perspective of a veteran who has warred with herself and survived. With unexpected moments of grace and flashes of humor, Sawchyn shows us the "body as a battleground of belonging" and offers this absorbing testament as an admirable addition to the literature of illness and recovery."

- ROBIN HEMLEY, AUTHOR OF *NOLA: A MEMOIR OF FAITH, ART, & MADNESS*

"Sawchyn has stacked her debut essay collection with stories she carried under her skin, tattoo-deep, until she could find a way to flip the needle and ink them onto the page. These are stories that waited—and then demanded to be told."

- JILL CHRISTMAN, AUTHOR OF *DARKROOM*

For my family, both by blood and by choice.

contents

An Apology 13

Wellness Index 25

Gutted 37

Notes from the Cliff Face 47

Inheritance 61

Deep-Sea Creatures 73

Three Men 87

Withdrawal 99

Go Ask Alice 113

Unsent 127

Indie Night at the Goth Club 135

Flight 145

Notes 155

Acknowledgments 159

... revelatory truth has a great allure: It seems to answer our craving for order and meaning. It gives our chaotic histories a satisfying "shapeliness."
– **Emily Fox Gordon,** *Mockingbird Years*

I think we are well-advised to keep on nodding terms with the people we used to be, whether we find them attractive company or not.
– **Joan Didion,** "On Keeping a Notebook"

an apology

This is how I ended up in the hospital: My mother found me sitting in my room, knees pulled into my chest, face pushed into my knees, arms wrapped around myself as far as they would go, rocking forward and back, muttering. I heard small murmurs that sounded like the second half of my name being whispered, soft whooshes from an idling gaming console that did not exist, saw peony bush branches swaying as marionette puppets through the window and garbage bags turn into fish swimming down the black river highway. I was eighteen. I was unwell. I held my body like other people hold worry stones or rosaries—for reassurance, to remind myself of what exists.

If I remember correctly, which I cannot guarantee, I tried to hit my mother when she reached out to touch me.

I don't think I've ever apologized for this. *past tense*

Though it's easy to push a quick *I'm sorry* through the lips, to apologize in the truest sense of the word is a difficult matter. The word *apology* comes from the French *apologie,* which, in turn, comes from the Greek ἀπολογία (*apologia*). Its roots are based in self-preservation; the etymological parent describes formal written or spoken statements of (usually self) defense.

Structure: Italics

Think of Plato's *The Apology of Socrates* where the philosopher attempts to vindicate himself of the supposed corruption of the city's youth. To apologize then, in the classical sense, requires an excellent memory, one that can recall with some detail past actions that require explanation. For example: *No, I did not mean to hit her; it was a reflex* or *It was an accident; I was waving her away.* Failing that, it requires the ability to persuade the listener of pure intentions: *I swear* or *I promise* or, most distressingly, *Trust me.*

present I have little faith in my motivations that night. There is a sliver of possibility I knew exactly what I was doing and was manipulative enough to use a breakdown as an excuse to let loose my rage at a target I knew would absorb its force instead of reflecting it back. Lacking certainty or self-understanding, I choose to say nothing. Insufficient apologies can be disastrous; Socrates' resulted in his drinking hemlock poison.

It's easy to couch my silence in etymology and historical context, to point backward thousands of years instead of sorting through the knot of emotions tangled like a dainty silver chain I put in my pocket and forgot about.

The first loop:

What frightens me most is that I may have misremembered, that I could apologize to my mother and she would respond with confusion. That I may have created a memory of hitting her is more troubling to me than the possibility of having actually done so (regardless of motivation) because it suggests I still harbor more resentment either toward her or myself than I'd like to believe.

There are a number of beginnings I feel I should remember but do not: first day of school, first kiss. Given full jurisdiction over what my brain holds in its crevices, I would allocate less space to song lyrics I am now embarrassed of. Instead, I am left with an organ that buries so many significant events and well-intentioned insights, but keeps at the ready the first time I heard the band Nirvana.

I sat in a dark high school auditorium with my friend, our knees pulled into our chests and feet resting on the seat cushions, trying to be small. We watched upperclassmen rehearse a modern dance performance. A girl somehow glided across the bright, polished wooden floor of the stage in tennis shoes, and the thrumming F, A#, G#, C# chords hit just the right synapses required for lasting memory, were compelling enough to override—at least temporarily—my teenage fear, which I have yet to fully outgrow, of seeming less-than-omniscient. I needed to know the song's name, the artist, something so that I could hear it again, only louder, with bass that dove into my body and made my blood vessels pulse.

I leaned over to my friend, whispered, "What is this?"

She answered.

"Oh yeah," I said, quickly acting as if it was something I'd known but forgotten, as if I just couldn't think of the title.

The doctors said it was *acute psychosis*. Diagnostically, the hypothetical swing at my mother was not my fault. I was sick, they said. *Bipolar I*, they said. This behavior of mine was part of a *manic episode* and could be expected, even predicted, according to this new terminology that would shape the next seven years of my life. author sounds unsure

Bipolar I. The phrase asserted that this (the whooshing sounds, the running fish shadows, the violence) would likely happen again. Unhinging from reality—manifested in a mood that swung down then back up, hanging mid-air like Wile E. Coyote just before he realizes he's gone off a cliff—was part of my body, my biology, and something to endure or manage with a lifetime of medication and behavior modification and therapy.

My memory of that night skips like a scratched record from me in my bedroom—the lashing out that may or may not have happened—to the emergency room. A nurse trying to slip in an IV found a forearm full of scars and still-open wounds. She asked if I wanted to hurt myself, if I were going to do it, how would I do it. I remember saying something flippant about *playing in traffic*, and, for years, that was the line of dialogue I gave myself when replaying my spotty memories of that night. It was only recently that I began to question the likelihood of my telling a joke at such a supposedly serious time.

But I should not be so suspicious of my eighteen-year-old self. If discussion of strong sentiment gives me pause now, pushing me into avoidant intellectualization or humor, surely I was equally awkward and even more graceless as a teenager. Surely.

Medical records confirm that I've always struggled with the right thing to say, albeit in clinical terms. My admission history from the hospital discharge paperwork reads: *The patient has . . . a recent plan to run in front of a car and kill herself.* So much for sarcasm. author has clear voice

Another skip, hours later: I woke up in the cliché locked room with padded walls. A small empty chair, plastic and metal, sized for an elementary-school student, stood sentry. Skip, skip, skip. My mother wanted me to stay in there. She felt badly for me, too, gave me her mother's pearl ring to wear and feel loved. But I would not stay.

I spent the next few nights sleeping in different places, returning to my parents' house through the garage door during the workday hours. One evening, I stood outside an IHOP smoking with the friend who'd picked me up from the psych ward. I watched my naked hand wave its cigarette through the air and panicked; I'd insisted on wearing the ring on my engagement finger, even though its gold band was too big, because I thought it made it look like I belonged with someone. I couldn't even fake that. My guts knotted up inside themselves.

I have apologized for this loss several times, but I do not think my efforts have resulted in forgiveness. My mother purses her lips, makes a sound with her tongue against the roof of her mouth that I recognize from my own body as an expression of deep disappointment. If anything, I suspect my apologies only bring up memories my mother would rather forget because they get in the way of her loving me. When I remember the lost jewelry, the *I'm sorry* belly-crawling out of my mouth, my stomach still twists into the same shape it did when I first saw my naked ring finger.

I am remorseful, perhaps disproportionately so. Given the ability to undo any past transgression, I would choose to recover that ring. It seems petty compared to the other damages I've inflicted, but it is also concrete, something I could hold in my hand and know with my eyes, my sense of touch. Considering how it has misled me in the past, I'm surprised how tightly I still hold on to my body as my means of understanding truth. Walking around my hometown, I sometimes imagine that glints on the sidewalk in the corner of my eye are the ring, somehow impossibly looping back to me so many years later. The fantasy continues before I turn my head to look: I return the ring to my mother, and she embraces me, insists I keep it, that I am a trustworthy person now. She smiles and warns me to now wear the ring on a larger finger, or maybe we drive to a jeweler to have it resized so I can wear it how I'd like because now I can at least act like I belong with someone.

But perhaps there are some transgressions that cannot be completely forgiven, no matter the instigator's intent or regret, and we must instead muddle on as best we can, acting as if we are whole.

The word *remorse* also comes from French, *remords*, in turn from the Latin *remordēre*. It means *to bite back* or, more accurately, *to bite again*. A remorseful person feels the nips of past bad behavior at her heels and is inspired to run faster, to run farther away from the actions that led to the feeling's inciting events. A slowed flight results in marks shaped like parentheses made of dashes around the Achilles tendon, could be crippling. The true penitent, reminded by such sharp teeth, is then unlikely to repeat mistakes.

In the case of the hypothetical swing and the missing jewelry, the plan of action moving forward reads as follows: Do not kick holes in the bedroom walls, do not bite fingernails, do not consume amphetamines, do not get caught hallucinating. And so on.

There's that push-back humor again—deflecting while asking the reader to do the imaginative work for me. Like you know what accompanies such bodily violence. Maybe you do.

The working end of the knot:

I have spent most of my adult life actively working my way out of a morass of teenage damage and institutionalizations. It's a slow and uninteresting process that's consisted of abstinence, critical self-reflection, begrudging acceptance, and restraint. It has made me feel boring and older than my age. But the alternative was to continue pretending I was able to run across wide-open canyons, pretending I'd never fallen down. My imagination was not fertile enough, my body not regenerative.

My friend in the auditorium had an older brother, a relationship of confidences with her mother, and beautiful red hair. She had so many things I wanted. She also played guitar. Though I had some classical training in strings, I was wretched at strumming. My friend was nonetheless a patient teacher.

We sat on the floor of her bedroom, and I borrowed her red-and-white Ibanez and practiced how tightly to hold a pick. She pointed out that this is the best guitar brand, the one Kurt Cobain used—this is patently untrue, though I believed her without question at the time.

Of course, one of the first songs I learned to play in full was "About a Girl," a Nirvana classic Cobain described in a *Rolling Stone* interview as a "jangly R.E.M. type of pop song." I was besotted with the chords, with his wailing. It sounded nothing like the pop I knew.

This girl was one of my first real friends who stayed with me through the years despite time and distance. After she taught me guitar, we drank liter pitchers of strawberry daiquiris, wandered around cities late at night, and snuck cigarettes and sprayed ourselves with too much perfume to cover it up. We stayed up all night against our own wishes, fighting and fueling insomnia with teenage angst. Of course, we formed a band, had a lot of feelings. *Cut myself on angel's hair and baby's breath.* This time with her was the first foothill of my upward climb that would eventually land me in a hospital, but all I knew then was that I was happy when I was with her and that we were almost the same.

Seven years after my diagnosis, I stopped taking my psychiatric medication and emerged from the long withdrawal process mostly unscathed. No more bipolar I.

It was a risk, the nurse practitioner pointed out to me; manic bipolar patients (which my medical records suggested I was) are notoriously resistant to taking their medication and my illness was *well-managed*. To deviate from *what's been working* could mean another step into a parallel universe, a journey through the kingdom of the sick. A flight that would end in confinement.

I wasn't certain at the beginning that the diagnosis was wrong. But I suspected. An idle curiosity winked inside me as I grew up, didn't return to the hospital, met other people whose entire bodies jangled with moods and illness on a daily basis. *Maybe*, I thought. The winking grew into the incessant sound of a smoke detector whose battery needs changing. *Fuck it. What's the worst that could happen?* I knew the answer but pushed the thought away.

My conversation with my mother then went something like this:

"I'm going to a doctor to see if I can stop taking my meds."

"Any particular reason?"

I made a sound like a shrug. She did not press.

After six months of tapering dosages, I was completely off my medication. When the withdrawal ended, I remained myself, both feet on mostly solid earth, having gained silent passage back into the kingdom of the well.

My mother and I have not discussed the implications of this misdiagnosis, what it means that the doctors were wrong, that I am fully culpable for my Schrödinger's fist. I am the girl who shouted in earnest, *The devil made me do it*, and then grew up to learn the devil isn't real, but, goddamn, growing up sure can look like madness.

So many of our words for unhappily looking back at the past come from the French. *Regret*, too, carries rolling Rs and francophile implications, *regreter* and *regretter*. These words' meanings are much the same as their English derivative—the feeling or expression of deep sadness after a loss, bewailing or lamenting. Regardless, the original words often implied an outward expression; it was not the sort of verb coddled and kept close to the chest, which is how I seem to prefer my emotions.

Few people knew that I took psychiatric medication, and so during and after the withdrawal process I kept the story and newfound knowledge mostly to myself. I imagined awkward conversations:

Hypothetical Person 1: How are things, Alysia?

Alysia: I recently weaned off all my psychiatric medication and found out I don't have bipolar disorder!

HP1: You had bipolar disorder?

A: Well, no, actually, but I thought I did.

Or,

Hypothetical Person 2: Anything new?

A: My identity was intertwined too tightly with a mental health diagnosis, and I am now reconceptualizing my self-understanding in light of a new framework.

HP2: . . .

The stigma of mental illness (and its attendant trope of the mentally ill woman writer) was heavy, but when I learned it had been a needless burden I felt guilty. As I saw it, my teenage behavior, so ferocious that white-coated professionals, who'd spent nearly a decade learning to properly categorize disorders, deemed me ill, had actually been a matter of poor choices, of riotous self-will.

Some questions I've actually been asked:

P1: You took the medication for *how* long?

A: Seven years.

And,

P2: How did the misdiagnosis happen?

A: I don't know—a lot of ways.

What I can and do imagine is usually worse than reality.

Another loop in the knot:

Though I did not want to be mentally ill as a teenager, I did want, very badly, an explanation for my destructive behavior. The symptoms fit. And as terrifying as the diagnosis was, with its inherent recurring hospitalizations, that certainty was more comfortable than a rainbowed and glittering miasma of not knowing, an oil slick of possibility. I'm ashamed to say the words *bipolar I* excused me, too, in part. I shoved off a small part of my agency and guilt onto an untraceable sickness that I could learn to *manage* but ultimately not *control*.

Kurt Cobain died at twenty-seven from a gunshot wound to the head, another addition to the infamous group of musicians and artists—Jimi Hendrix, Janis Joplin, Brian Jones, Jim Morrison—who passed away tragically at the same age. Though officially ruled a suicide, there are a number of ardent fans, my guitar-playing friend included, who maintain that Cobain's widow, Courtney Love, is responsible for his death. I'm unsure how they remain certain of the actions (or inactions) of a man they did not know personally.

The last single released before Cobain's death was a track titled "All Apologies." As Nirvana songs go, this one is melodic, soothing. At a concert some time before the song's official circulation, Cobain dedicated its performance to his wife and daughter, though he denied that the song was written about them. Its final refrain: *All in all is all we are.*

If Cobain really did kill himself and if the dedication to his family suggests this song is one of importance that expresses something he was never able to voice directly or in person, I think I may understand the man more than I'd expected, more than I'd like to, because I have spent over a year writing these pages—teasing out meaning from etymology and syntax—instead of sitting down with my mother and having a conversation.

My mother, when growing up, was taught not to voice her apologies. Instead, the way to indicate remorse was to avoid eye contact with the wronged party, to slip out of rooms when they entered them, to not speak. True contrition was recognized by absence rather than actions. Accordingly, a person demonstrated forgiveness by one day acknowledging the ghost, speaking and acting as if nothing had happened, a return to normalcy after a period of silence.

Perhaps I've inherited my reticence toward overt apologies; my avoidant impulses are simply a byproduct of my upbringing rather than fear. Whatever the cause, making amends is hard. My brain has swallowed or dissolved days and months. I do not know what needs an apology. I sometimes wonder if my memories from that time are actually hushed secondhand stories, repeated after the fact, eavesdropped from two rooms away.

The good news is that if for my mother to forgive means acting as if nothing has happened, then I have been forgiven for everything. A few months before my twenty-seventh birthday I visited my childhood home, tried to sleep in the same basement bedroom where I saw shadow puppets, punched through the drywall, and heard hushed sweeping sounds a decade prior. I stayed up too late, headphones in, stared at the ceiling, considered the likelihood of the house being razed the coming summer and with it my memories. Cobain wailed in my ears. The next morning, my mother asked *si j'ai bien dormie, si je veux un verre d'eau*. She brought me a cup of tea.

wellness index

Alice's *Adventures in Wonderland*: A children's book by mathematician Charles Lutwidge Dodgson (Lewis Carroll), adapted for film by Walt Disney in 1951. Start here. It is embarrassing to still love something that appears on Hot Topic t-shirts, but be honest: This is the book that cycles through your life, appearing again and again. Grace Slick sings, "One pill makes you larger and one pill makes you small / and the ones that mother gives you / don't do anything at all." Salvador Dali's girl jumps rope through your dreams. Johnny Depp as Hunter S. Thompson places the cassette player on the sink instead of hurling it into the bathtub. Your friend's newest manuscript includes the quote, *The proper definition of a man is an animal that writes letters.* At night, right before you fall asleep, your tongue feels like it's growing growing growing— your teeth fold over beneath its expansion like small paper tickets. What power it should have at this size.

Bipolar I: An illness distinguished by its highs and well suited for volatile dramas, films with light and shadow. Moods and energy shoot upward with enough force to clear the atmosphere and gravity's pull. In a rush of mania, you headed for the stars and their distant lights; you talked too fast, slept and ate too little, were reckless with your body and felt good about it. During manic episodes (particularly at their onset) individuals are hard-pressed to realize something is amiss because of the jackpot feeling that accompanies the excess energy. It's like being superhuman or on just the right amount of cocaine. Imagine: motivation and energy, regardless of hours slept or gallons of green juice consumed; preternatural inspiration, a muse perched on the shoulder humming catchy show tunes; heightened awareness, *jamais vu*, the first time diving into a pile of fall leaves or trying coffee ice cream. This is how it starts.

C ounseling, regular: Dialogue sessions designed to help patients gain self-awareness and modify troublesome behaviors. It was easy at first. Your therapist pulled out an astrology book and asked for your birthday, and you spent every other Tuesday talking about your childhood, about the people you were having sex with. Five years later, it changed. It = your insurance, your therapist, the city in which you lived, everything. Counseling was expensive in the heartland. In order to justify its cost you had to leave a man, precipitated by an excoriation of the soul, a coming clean.

D epo-Provera (generic, depo medroxyprogesterone acetate): An injected contraceptive. Unlike birth control pills, which you took for three years before a pharmacist said, quietly, "Uhm, excuse me?" as you picked up your prescriptions, Depo does not interfere with the liver's processing of psychiatric medication. Though you typically went to a doctor's office to have the shot administered, an extended period of travel meant an exception and the pharmacy gave you two syringes. The medication is intramuscular and necessitates a distressingly long needle. You pretended, both times, there was heroin in the barrel. It was the only way to convince yourself to plunge the metal into your flesh. A puncture wound seemed so much more distressing than a burn, a slash, a hunger, any other kind of violence—there have been so many—you have done to your body.

Electroconvulsive Therapy: The passage of small electric currents through the brain, prescribed to alleviate severe mental illness when medication, counseling, and behavioral modification are insufficient. You imagined this was barbaric stuff (a leather bit between the teeth, human like a horse, muscles rippling as electricity gallops through the body), straight out of those books that you held close to your heart and that shaped your ideas about sanity: *One Flew Over the Cuckoo's Next*, *Girl Interrupted*, *The Bell Jar*. They made you grateful for today's cornucopia of pills and pills and pills. Of course, you imagined incorrectly. The woman you lived with said there is no pain, only emptiness: a rubber eraser pushed through the past. She is made of stronger stuff than you.

Focalin XR (generic, dexmethylphenidate hydrochloride): A stimulant prescribed for attention deficit disorder. XR indicates "extended release." Its capsules should not, but can, be split open. When tipped onto a hard surface, crushed under a stiff ID into a powder, and snorted, its beaded innards burn. Once you learned to take the medication as prescribed, your heart beat with the force of a boxer's fist hitting a punching bag. You watched your pulse like a metronome above your left breast. This seemed unfair: Your body rejected the pills after you stopped treating them like candy, and so you had to go without. Your mouth then moved before your mind could stop it, generally in laughter that startled with its force, but doesn't everyone's? No?

G od, or if you prefer,

H igher Power: You prefer neither. Certain communities posit that belief in a spiritual force larger than the self provides a de-centering that can alleviate (*relieve*) mood swings and chemical dependency. You tried hard to have faith in something, an entity or energy vast enough to matter yet still concerned with those daily minutiae that seem catastrophic in the moment but are ultimately irrelevant on the scale of your life. You prayed, a volley of *uhms* and *you knows* and *this is stupid* and *fuck* and *fuck* and *fuck*, until you didn't. You find faith not in the firmament, but in the goodness of humans. Though this sometimes seem even less plausible than a man in the sky.

I nstitutionalization, voluntary and otherwise: Recommended during times of intense mania or depression as it provides individuals with a secure (*confined*) environment. Though psychiatric facilities are ideally places of recovery, this was not your experience. Despite all the movies you'd watched, all the books you'd read, you were unprepared for the experience of it. To say that the psych ward felt like a black hole feels both hyperbolic and expected, but you do not know of any other force that is so obliterating. It was like being reduced to dust; left there long enough, your atoms would be rearranged at a level so small you wouldn't recognize any part of yourself in the end.

Junk: A slang term for heroin immortalized in William S. Burroughs' *Junky*. Everywhere you've lived the drug is more popularly called smack or dope. There is a romance to it that pulls at you, as evidenced by your taste in junkie-skinny men. Heroin chic—their stomachs muscled from a lack of body fat, abdominals dipping in the shape of an arrow, the depression just wide enough for a finger, a tongue. Usually the descriptor was warranted.

Klonopin (generic, clonazepam): A benzodiazepine pre-scribed for both general anxiety and panic attacks. These pills are quick-acting and delicious. Swallowing them felt like prescription sunglasses over your whole body. The doctor at the psych ward released you with a 30-day prescription that you finished much earlier than he intended. The small insecurities that caught you throughout the day and kept you up at night (a joke gone awry; the gnawing certainty that you are not liked, only humored; a moment you forgot to smile) dissolved beneath the pills' protection. The larger devils (the people you once loved; the hurts you have inflicted; the terror of impermanence) only waved smiling from afar. You stopped taking the pills because they are your favorite. You wanted stay like that forever, washed in blue.

Lamictal (generic, lamotrigine): An anticonvulsant created for epileptic seizures that is now often used to treat bipolar disorder. After much trial and error, you were prescribed a starter kit. It took two months instead of one to get up to therapeutic dosage because you are bad at following directions—even the task of swallowing once a day proved too much. The irony was obvious to you even then: Years spent consuming anything that might change the way you felt, but you balked and forgot with this prescription. The pill was shaped like a diamond. Maybe you were afraid it would sap your personality. Maybe the energy felt good. The medication built up in your blood like a fortress around your misfiring neurotransmitters. Your moods evened out. You did not return to the psych ward. Eventually, you became so well, you wondered if you needed the medicine anymore.

Meditation, varied: Breathing techniques used to calm the mind. Delivery methods include CDs, various talks around the Eastern seaboard, podcasts, the sound of your own breath, and an ill-conceived ashram retreat. You don't like to talk about this—your experiences lose all dignity when spoken aloud. It began with a two-minute timer on your phone, while your open eyes darted around the room. You gnawed at the skin around your fingers. It took years to sit with the void yawning inside your chest long enough to make its presence throughout the day bearable. Your tolerance for its company is still in flux.

Nirvana: Creators of the song "Lithium," named for the first major medication developed to treat bipolar disorder. Side effects include disorientation, producing a *lithium shuffle* in patients; dry mouth; and sudden urges to urinate. You were never prescribed this, which seemed like a missed opportunity for synchronicity, given your taste in music. Though maybe it was for the best—one less compound to puzzle your liver—as seven years after the psych ward, another doctor pronounced you *misdiagnosed*.

Oxcarbazepine (brand name, Trileptal): Another anti-convulsant prescribed for bipolar disorder. You took this in a treatment facility where phlebotomists came into your room while you slept. In the mornings, you woke with discrete Band-Aids over your right elbow ditch. They were checking your sodium levels; a common side effect of Trileptal is their subsequent plummeting, which manifests in nausea and a decreased appetite. *Put some extra salt on your food,* advised the doctor with cartoonish facial hair. You couldn't tell if he was joking, but he switched your pills for something else.

Prozac (generic, fluoxetine): A selective serotonin re-uptake inhibitor (SSRI) antidepressant used for bipolar disorder in conjunction with a mood stabilizer. One pill plus another pill. Without this pairing, Prozac can exacerbate or cause manic symptoms in bipolar patients. Every night, you had detailed, movie-length dreams and woke up tired. Prozac, and SSRIs in general, can also provide depressed patients with the energy to act out their suicidal ideations before the feel-good kicks in. You only played at killing yourself. Some of these pills. Some leftover Crown whiskey. It wasn't enough, and you knew it. You offered up your hurt like a gift of flowers to anyone who would look at you.

Quetiapine (brand name, Seroquel): A mood-stabilizer featured in Lil Wyte's song "Oxy Cotton" as a com-panion to the titular drug—*But I pop 'em with Seroquel like glue.* Your doctor prescribed it for sleep but if it evened you out a bit that couldn't hurt. One night, as Spanish moss waved in the autumn breeze, you forgot to take your pills at the regular time and your hands shook. Your eyelids fluttered, heavy like a nod. You'd been clean for maybe a year, but it was the same sensation as when you'd taken too many (just enough) opiates and a dull feeling of *more* crawled through your arms. *This is not*, you thought, *supposed to happen anymore.*

Retrospective: To look back, to survey, to examine what came before. When you think about time, do you envision a circle? A woman with hazel eyes told your fortune using your birthday; the numbers 8/8 signified the interior and exterior of your life matching, a wheel spinning and dragging you through the experiences of *pauper and prince.* Or is time linear? Another woman asked if you envision the past behind you and the future in front, or the past to the left and the future to the right. You chose the latter; if the present is the midline of the body, most events receding past your left shoulder are blurred and more pleasant for the perspective. She said this means you are always looking back. This is true. It's how meaning is made: Small stars wink across the light-years to form constellations from Earth.

Sleep, regular: Maintaining consistent sleep habits can both reduce the severity and slow the onset of manic and depressive states. You told all your doctors, *I have never slept well.* As a child, your bedroom window faced east, and you opened the blinds and watched the moon make her way across your soft pink blanket. As an adult, you find clarity while everyone else sleeps—those hours few people experience consciously, the gap between late night and early morning.

Trazodone (brand name, varies): An SSRI for major depressive disorder also prescribed as a sleep aid. It was underwhelming. You took it without complaint, but it didn't put you out at night the way you wanted (with the force of a blow to the brain). This is the trouble with your desires: The pills that knock you out leave you rubber-limbed and uneasy, that too-familiar feeling; the pills that don't are worthless. To give up desire is the greatest trick of all.

Unsolicited Advice: Usually from acquaintances, arrives in both question and statement form (*Have you tried X? / You should try Y*), and is often accompanied by a far-removed credential (*My friend's mom's cat-walker read this article that says Z*). Your first small pleasure at the revelation of your misdiagnosis was not that you would remain free of the psych ward, but rather that all those people who thought they knew what was best for you were wrong wrong wrong. Years later, you noticed the depths of your bitterness only when you began to leave its murky waters, glints of sunlight slanting through the shallows. A breath of air, a fish growing lungs.

Valproic acid (brand name, Depakote): Another combination anticonvulsant/mood stabilizer. Your friend took it. Your ex-boyfriend took it. Your other friend took it. They were slow in their speech and offered heavy silences before they responded to your questions. You often spoke too much in their presence. (Though perhaps they were just more considerate than you, responsive rather than reactive, and it had nothing to do with the pills.) Your ex-boyfriend had a permanently bemused expression. Sometimes you thought about punching him in the arm. You wondered if it would hurt, somewhere beneath all those sealed-up milligrams.

Welbutrin (generic, buproprion): A non-SSRI antidepressant with possible side effects of increased energy, a general sense of well-being, and a decreased appetite. The medication is not recommended for individuals with eating disorders. You did not have depression, but you did have disordered eating, and you sometimes wished your doctors were incompetent enough to prescribe this to you so that you could more easily become whittled down to your bones and disappear. Some things do not change, at their root: a wish to swallow something and escape yourself.

Xanax (generic, alprazolam): A benzodiazepine with a faster release and shorter half-life than Klonopin. Xanax is often prescribed on an as-needed basis, rather than as daily maintenance for anxiety—think *black oblivion* instead of *blue peace*. The panic attacks started the autumn you weaned off your mood stabilizers (side effects may include). You went back to a doctor, desperate, and said, *Help me, please, but do not give me this. This I cannot manage.*

Yoga (Ashtanga, hatha, Iyengar, vinyasa): Broadly, a total system for living with origins in ancient India. In the United States, contemporary yoga classes are mostly physical and focus on pairing movement with breath. It took you a long time to learn even this stripped-down version. You contorted your body into shapes it was not ready for. The point is to meet your body where it is. To learn to distinguish discomfort from pain. The point is to hold the poses, so that you may hold similar unease in life. To breathe through the desire to disappear.

Ziprasidone (brand name, Geodon): An antipsychotic prescribed for schizophrenia and bipolar mania. You could not stand. You could not stay awake. You sat down on tile floors covered in coffee grounds. You sat down while taking drive-thru orders. You nodded off at the bus stop. You napped at other people's houses. You stopped taking the pills, despite your doctor's assurances that their side effects would fade. You said, *No.* It took many years to apply this agency to the rest of your life, to the rest of the medicines and regimens that didn't help but you tried anyway because you wanted to be normal and okay and whole and good. This was the beginning.

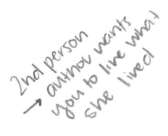

2nd person
↗ author wants
you to live what
she lived

gutted

The girl is a picky eater. She doesn't do it on purpose—once inside her mouth, peas grow and shoot tendrils down the back of her throat, tickling her gag reflex; sharp cheeses slice through her tongue and leave her unable to taste anything but their spoiled tang for weeks.

When I met the first man I loved, I was not eating.

In truth, I was eating, but I wasn't eating much. I prefer the sound of the first sentence, though. It is cleaner, tighter. It is easier to understand.

The summer before my senior year of high school, I was prescribed a Ritalin derivative.

Every morning, I ran upstairs to my parents' bathroom, peed, took off my clothes, and stepped on the scale. It was impossible not to notice my weight loss, and I imagined I was the envy of every girl in my class that fall.

Many days, I only drank orange juice while the sun was up. Weeknights, I ate a sham dinner with my parents. It was a stressful, ritualistic affair. We ate at a hardwood table off plates edged in two-tone blue zigzags. There was salad, there was meat, there was starch, there were vegetables. Fork on the left, knife and spoon on the right. We had napkin holders. My mother garnished the food with parsley.

These were difficult meals. Not because of the propriety or formality, but because they were the only times my parents and I spent together and tried to get along without the motivation of others' expectations and eyes to keep us civil. I ate fast. I answered questions sparsely, like so many other teenagers, with monosyllabic responses like *good* and, especially, *fine*, the i-sound alternately clipped or drawn-out depending on whether I was expressing avoidance or exasperation.

That summer, despite the variety of food on the table, I ate only salad and small amounts of protein. No starch or dressing or dairy touched my plate.

"You look great," they said.

One night, my mother made mussels with cream and cut an entire baguette into hearty, thick chunks, arranging them on a cloth napkin in a woven basket. She placed the basket between me and my father, knowing how much we loved the warm, chewy slices. I ate one piece.

"You have such wonderful self-control," my father said.

When I stepped on the scale the next morning, I felt guilt and shame.

I was disappearing and becoming more visible at the same time. As I tucked my hands around my hip bones at night, I envisioned impurities and character flaws being burned away with my baby fat. As my cheekbones caught the light in the mornings, I was a sculpture, all stone. I imagined I could feel my stomach walls touching themselves and felt strong, like I was superhuman, surviving on air.

I now know this is child's play for an anorexic. This only lasted until the spring, less than a full year, when I was eventually coerced by a man with a pockmarked face into eating bits of dried squid, handfuls and handfuls of clementines, hearty pasta dishes. I stayed thin, though I wouldn't think so until years later.

The girl's parents grow desperate: They set a timer in front of her and threaten to throw away all unfinished food at the shrill alarm. One night, she outright refuses to eat the tinned salmon placed in front of her, and her father sends her to bed without dinner. But he relents. He brings her applesauce and apologies. She is an only child.

Almost everyone I know has a first love story and almost all these stories end badly. I'm pretty sure the first man I fell hard for, Xavier, had some nonspecific Asian fetish. Think pornography tastes and historical fiction and katanas lining his bedroom walls. Though distressing in retrospect, it felt good at the time because I thought it meant he would stay mine.

Our families had only one obvious characteristic in common: We ate dinner together most nights at our respective dining room tables.

On Fridays and Saturdays, my nighttime meals migrated from my parents' house to Xavier's. Dinners there were entirely different, long and pleasantly drawn-out—an hour to eat, another hour for coffee and cigarettes. Even the light at his house was softer, all incandescent bulbs and candles. His mother cooked in enamelware that came out of the oven and went directly onto the tabletop. Xavier and his younger brother bickered and play-wrestled over whose turn it was to do the dishes. The dim light got dimmer as four of us— Xavier's father, his mother, him, and me—sat around the long table. We talked for hours.

My own mother and father, of course, strongly disliked Xavier and his family. There was a leniency there, absent in my own household, that concerned my parents.

"They smoke in the house," said my father, who had quit only five years before.

"It's cultural." My mother spooned stir-fried vegetables onto my plate, then hers. "The Dutch, they let their children run wild. You know?"

I shrugged.

"They let their children make mistakes," she said. A grimace.

My father picked cucumbers out of the salad with his fingers.

A full five words, one conjunction, exited my mouth. "What's so bad about that?"

My mother shook her head, tsked her tongue against the back of her front teeth.

"You can just tell when a family is Dutch," she said.

Though my mother couched her dislike of Xavier's parents in cultural differences, a part of it was jealousy, though she would not admit this until years later. As I moved further and further away from my family, I moved closer and closer to his. And though now we can almost write it off as another trial of late adolescence, I wonder if my mother feared a pattern emerging, if, given her physical distance from her own family, she worried the growing rift between us would culminate in a cross-continental move, like mother like daughter.

There was also this: Xavier went days without shaving because the stubble hid acne scars on his face. He was junkie-skinny from heroin. Either despite or because of these qualities, I cherished him all the more. My body still felt small against his.

•

"You know what my mother told me?" the girl's mother asks.

The girl shakes her head. Her grandmother, her mother's mother, speaks only in Chinese, and the girl cannot understand anything she says.

"She told me to always eat all my rice. She told me each grain left in the bowl would be a mark on my future husband's face." Her mother reaches across the table, runs her hand across the girl's father's face. "See what nice skin he has?" she asks. "I always finished my rice."

Xavier moved to the Netherlands to attend college. He lived, for a time, in the upstairs room of an artist's house. Located in a small, picturesque town, the house was an old converted printing studio. The artist, Elena, had removed walls, installed those ubiquitous European windows that opened sideways and from the top depending on how the handles were turned. Xavier said when she first showed him his room, there were bunches of marijuana hanging from the rafters.

"Sorry," she'd said. "We've been using the place for storage."

He moved in immediately.

Elena and her partner, Thomas, were wonderful, warm people. She painted with oils and rented rooms. He lived on a houseboat and worked as a hospice nurse. Though Xavier had since moved to a different city to be closer to school, we spent several days at her home when I visited him one early March.

Elena, Thomas, Xavier, and I stayed up late, sitting around a long plastic table in the kitchen. We rarely ate dinner, but I hardly felt hungry. I smoked cigarette after cigarette, drank purple Fanta, and felt like our time around the table was all that existed of life, that the school and work I'd left behind were disappearing, had never really mattered. We listened to music, talked about work, politics, art, about anything. As the hours swam by, we waltzed in various pairs, sometimes human and mop, around the room, humming. Elena rolled the weed she'd grown in her garden into each cigarette she smoked with dexterous, artist's fingers. Crates of beer disappeared. One night, when Xavier and I walked to the store to buy more, the cashier, a petite blonde, flirted with him. I didn't need to speak the language to understand her gestures, her eyes. I teased him about it back at the kitchen table.

"Don't do that," Elena said, pointing at me.

"I'm kidding," I said.

"Doesn't matter." Her blue eyes were red and half-lidded. "You know he loves you, so you shouldn't say it. And if he didn't, you saying something wouldn't make a difference."

She was right.

Friends came by the house. One night, it was a group of men from Xavier's university.

Another night, it was Everhart. I'm not sure what he did at the time, but he'd said he was part of the U.N. peacekeeping mission during the Kosovo War. Half caricature, he remarked how pleasantly surprised he was that, though American, I was not grossly overweight. Later, he told me a story about drowning a litter of motherless kittens in a war zone "for their own good, you understand?" He sang slow Dutch ballads and riotous, political French songs.

The day I left, Elena burned her yard waste, all the dead leaves and plants from the winter, in a small iron stove in the backyard. It gave off enough heat for us to sit outside comfortably while the sun was up. Thomas cooked breakfast, fried eggs and meat, made sandwiches of dark, thick bread served with mugs and mugs of coffee. I picked around the yolks.

Everhart was still there, though I'm not sure if or where he slept. Xavier brought his camera outside and took photographs of everyone while we weren't paying attention. The pictures' backgrounds look faded from the pervasive white smoke. Thomas' blond ponytail is a blur, Elena's eyes are half-closed, her mouth open. Everhart looks directly at the camera. In most of the photos of me, I am in motion—laughing, talking, my hands a tan smudge in front of my face as I bring a cigarette to my mouth. There is one, though, where I am still. I am sitting on the ground, wearing Xavier's sweater. It is too big for my thin frame, the soft material hangs off my shoulders, casting deep shadows around my collarbones. My hair is dark and pulled back, and I am holding a coffee mug so big my hands barely touch when wrapped around it.

When I got back from the trip, my parents did not ask if I had a good time. They were annoyed I'd chosen to go in the first place, that I hadn't yet grown out of or away from this man. Years later, when they saw the picture of me holding the too-large coffee mug and another of me smiling, sitting at Elena's kitchen table, they asked where they were taken and by whom. They said I looked so happy, so thin, so rested there. I don't remember if I answered.

Xavier tried to take a photograph of himself to give to me, but his attempts never came out right. In some pictures he looks nervous, like he is about to run away, like the light is too much for his pale eyes. In others, he looks like he is mid-sigh. His cheeks are speckled. So many tiny shadows scatter his face from the March afternoon light.

What the girl does like are clementines. She can eat pounds of them in a sitting. She enjoys the task of peeling the small, thin-skinned fruits, taking the rind off in one piece—a process that initially required much concentration, but one she now does automatically. Afterward, she curls the skins back in place, trying to align the tears as best she can, so the peel is reassembled, empty, like a snakeskin shed and left behind. She sometimes swallows the peeled fruits whole and pretends she is unhinging her jaw. The girl is a python, her stomach stretches, pushes out. She will finish them all.

Some habits take years to kick: Later in life, I moved to a land-locked state where I lived with yet another man with bad skin. Luke was a picky eater, native to the region and named for one of its original evangelists. I cooked, but he was suspicious of my bone-in meats, seafood, and rainbow of produce. I learned to make potatoes and potatoes and potatoes, savory pies with cream, huge pans of chili with cornbread. I gained weight from the heavy starches; my clothes fit snugly for the first time since I was a teenager, and my heaviness kept me warm through the Midwestern winters.

Luke and his best friend went fishing at a lake one afternoon. They caught maybe twenty fish between them—a mix of crappie (pronounced *craw-pee*) the small, patterned sunfish coveted in Midwestern lakes, and smallmouth bass. When they returned home, Luke stayed in the living room, disgusted, while his friend taught me the motions of separating meat from a body, of peeling skin, of teasing out spines and ribs. It was time-consuming, and my hands moved awkwardly around the once-living creatures.

Most of the fish were female. Luke's friend pulled yellow egg sacs out of their bellies with his thick fingers.

"Don't puncture these," he said. "You can fry 'em up if they stay whole."

The caught fish were piled outside on the balcony, still in a net, and after an hour of gutting the heap seemed no smaller. They didn't smell. I wasn't sure why we kept them out there, but it turns out that sometimes, after being out of the water for hours, fish will convulse. They move as if they are alive. I was holding one's head in my hand when she seized, bending back and forth over herself like a silver slinky.

I yelped, high and loud.

Luke's friend, who was heating oil on the stove, stepped in front of me, picking up the knife I'd dropped on the counter, and hit the fish in the head with the butt of its handle. He stopped her movement, but also ruptured her eyeball. Clear goop clung to the underside of the faux-wood cabinets. I nearly put my hands to my mouth, but was stopped by the slime on my fingers.

When I was finished, Luke's friend made us dinner. The oil was hot, and the fish pieces were golden.

"Like chicken nuggets," Luke said.

His friend gave me a freezer bag full of the fish I'd cut, but Luke said he wouldn't eat them anymore, that he'd had enough.

I called my mother, told her I'd finally learned to clean fish.

The next weekend, Luke left town for work. On Friday night, I transferred the frozen filets from the freezer to the fridge to thaw. The next day, I poured rice into the cooker, rinsed the grains, used the knuckles on my middle finger to determine how much water was needed. I bought ginger, scallions, soy sauce, green onions. I steamed the fish with pleasure.

When it was all done, when the whole house smelled like my childhood kitchen, I scooped rice into a bowl and spooned the white, flaky fish on top. I ate sitting on the couch, feet up on the coffee table, no ceremony. Halfway through the meal, I paused and leaned back, deep into the cushions. In this deep slouch, I pulled my shirt up to uncover my belly.

I had been unkind to my body in the heartland. My stomach curved outward, like an inverted bowl, my hip bones hid beneath flesh. I finished the rice regardless.

notes from the cliff face

Autumn in Shenandoah National Park is the kind of sucker-punch scenery on which this country was founded. From mountaintops, the world undulates outward in smaller crests and hills like an untidy blanket. Hawks catch updrafts and tumble like seals in the ocean. Those same winds buffet the cheeks, and the air up here is ten degrees colder than it is at the mountain's base. Vegetation is thin. Thighs and scraped palms burn with equal insistence, a demand for attention that pulses alongside the heartbeat. We have arrived.

Drugs turn us into chameleons. They make a body well when it isn't, sick when it's healthy. Extended cocaine use looks like mania and psychosis: sleep deprivation, impulsivity, irritability, delusion, risk-taking, paranoia. For this reason, especially during an individual's first admittance into a psychiatric facility, it is important to clean them out and obtain a substance-use history before making a definitive mental health diagnosis.

I spent years intentionally toeing a line between *interesting* and *ruinous* and was bound to cross over with great flair at some point. I like cliffs because they are a physical representation of a sharp change—solid earth to air—where the planet's seemingly dependable foundations have been broken and will likely break again.

My first hike was the nine-mile trek up and down Old Rag Mountain, elevation 2,510 feet with rock scramble. The National Park Service lists the trail as Shenandoah's most dangerous and popular. Old Rag as my first hike might have been reasonable if I were an avid rock climber or a long-distance runner or not a pack-a-day smoker, but none of those things were true. I assured my hiking companion I would be *just fine*.

It is difficult to obtain accurate substance-use histories. Drug addicts lie.

The cocaine in Virginia looked like it does in movies: a rock that broke apart easily under the right sort of pointed pressure. White like snow but not like snow. More like cheap acrylic paint. Bigger granules than baking powder or washing soda. More like Borax. But not like that either.

I pulled on a knee-length skirt and men's hiking boots the morning of my first trek up Old Rag. I'd bought the shoes last-minute; they were the cheapest display pair at a small sporting goods store. I looked more ready for a New England music festival than a mountain range.

Drug addicts lie to themselves because addiction only ends in devastation. On the way down, there are occasional supernova moments of connection and maybe even compassion borne out of slingshot neurotransmitters and a lack of sleep and food. A camaraderie builds among addicts, *us against the world*. Near-disasters accompanied by rushing adrenaline can imbue every exhale with gratitude for life and its wonders. But it is ultimately devouring—consumption at the cost of everything else. In order to continue, we must tell ourselves our addiction will not swallow us. We must tell many smaller lies in the service of this larger one.

Getting out to Old Rag is a journey itself. From the Washington, D.C. suburbs, we drove for hours through the Shenandoah foothills in a diesel-drinking Volvo. Conversation slowed as we crawled up the roads, my friend's attention fixed on the curving asphalt and mine on the view. The sun had come up self-assured that morning, and the day felt bright with meaning. I hummed out the window at the cliff drops. Something inside me soared, but my hands were sweating and my knees got loose at the same time.

Drug addicts also forget, both by accident and on purpose. The latter is itself a type of lie.

My stock memory of doing cocaine in Virginia is not of the sex or the music or the violence or the car rides or the woods. It is of being the last person awake in a room full of passed-out junkies and typing emails at a computer with a background image cycling through psychedelic abstracts and half-naked women. To see 7 a.m. twice without sleep in between is a special sort of loneliness. The blackout curtains blocked out the dawn but not the suburban bird calls. I picked through smoked cigarette butts in a frying pan.

In high school, one of my favorite books was William S. Burroughs' *Junky*. The text validated my belief (hope) that the choices I was making to wear down my body fast would ultimately result in something beautiful. Though it's been years since I read the book, I still have a cozy feeling around my diaphragm when I think about it. I would like to revisit the text, but if I wish to keep the sensation, I am certain I should not.

My pride propelled me up the mountain. The first few hours of Old Rag's trail are steep switchbacks, one after the other. Imagine Sisyphus, but the boulder was my body. My friend's strides were long and loping, and though he carried our shared pack, my lungs shivered in the changing altitude. My skirt caught on branches. I took small sips of air. My lips dried out. My head buzzed.

I thought to be a Real Writer I had to do drugs. I thought I had to do them often and in solitude until they became a significant part of my identity, which would (obviously) be entwined with my creative process. This would result in some minor catastrophe, not resulting in permanent damage, just enough to intrigue. But the best laid plans of—wait, how does it go?

Cocaine works on the brain's rewards center, specifically its dopamine reabsorption. The neurotransmitter is released in response to pleasure. Ace an exam? Dopamine. Play with a puppy? Dopamine. Eat ice cream? Dopamine. Shoot up?

·

After one false summit and then another, we saw the sign announcing our arrival at Old Rag's peak. We took off our shoes and socks, and my toes felt new. I tucked my skirt between my knees. We ate our lunches on a boulder overlooking the green valley, and my breathing returned. *Billow*, I thought. *Ripple. Wave.* From this height, the hills we'd driven through and then climbed looked perfect, inevitable, necessary. My skinned palms worthwhile.

I never shot up. I used to wish I had, but that seems now like an impossibility that would have changed the trajectory of my entire life. I don't mean to sound dramatic. My at-the-time-boyfriend had veins that stood out whenever he made a fist. His forearms were snaked with faint turquoise rivers. It was his bedroom that had the blackout curtains. I thought I would marry him. I could never tell when he was on dope and when he wasn't because his voice always softened around my name.

Drug addicts lie to one another because getting fucked up becomes a competition. Not as in who-can-get-higher but as in there-are-a-finite-number-of-resources, primarily money. We're taught to share as children, but generosity is scarce on the cliff face. Sometimes a person comes into a bunch of cash or dope and there will be outpourings of affection, but these are exceptional instances. What do we have to offer, anyway, but further chiseling away at the self, moving a little closer to nothing?

•

Junkie memory is unreliable, too, because the lifestyle is chaotic, haphazard, unexpected. To answer, *Where?* is easier than, *When?* or, *Why?* I moved from state to state—Virginia, North Carolina, Virginia, Florida—as if the local flora or topography were causing the devastation, like a woman climbing a mountain to escape gravity.

I woke to my calves knotting themselves into bowlines the night after I climbed Old Rag. I couldn't walk without whimpers slipping from my mouth. I didn't think I would hurt that bad, and it took me a long time to admit it.

The cocaine in North Carolina was sticky and yellowish. It clung to the sides of my college ID / razor blade / baggie / driver's permit / cigarette cellophane / X-Acto knife with a tenacity that surprised. I joked it was the southern humidity that made it so.

Drug addicts lie to other people because they will try to stop us from doing what we want, which is to self-destruct in a manner that causes massive amounts of collateral damage. To be cared for is often to be tied to, and so we tear the links that bind us to others.

I told my boyfriend I wasn't hungover in between bouts of puking orange stomach bile into an empty cereal box.
    Why are you sick? he asked.
    I don't know, I said.

He called me a junkie, and I held the word close to my chest where it bloomed into thorns. We knew this meant we would now lie in equal amounts to one another.

I'd like to say I learned a lesson from that first hike. And I did learn *a* lesson, but I'm not sure it was the right one. Two years later, I hiked Old Rag again. That second time, I wore pants.

There was an all-hours Harris Teeter in North Carolina, and I was often there during those hours that are difficult to classify (is it late night or early morning?) buying a tin of Altoids as an excuse to withdraw cash. When they cleaned the store, it smelled like cocaine. It must have been some common, industrial-grade product. Years later, I round corners in supermarkets and inhale, unsuspecting, and everything rushes back.

I admitted to the psych ward doctors that I did drugs but said it wasn't a problem. I'd failed out of college, moved back in with my parents; it was a period of adjustment, limited in scope, a deviation from the normal. To say otherwise was to concede to something I wasn't ready for.

After we'd implicitly agreed to lie to one another, my boyfriend called me from the scene of a car accident. I sat barefoot on a patch of grass, listening. Our friend's first DUI, my boyfriend's face slammed into the dashboard, front teeth knocked out, a bloody mouth. Halfway through the conversation he sounded far away, and then nothing. A new voice spoke into my ear, a paramedic, explaining the whole thing in easier-to-understand language. The other people were okay. The boyfriend got new teeth.

I wore pants on that second hike, but I went by myself.

My first short stories were predictable, barely fictionalized narratives of the drug-riddled dead. I wouldn't admit how closely they cleaved to my life, and when I reread them now, I struggle to parse truth from fabrication. Everything whispers, *Possible*.

Cocaine does not taste good, but when I try to remember in order to describe it accurately here, I salivate.

Two pairs of hikers sandwiched my second hike up Old Rag. They appeared and disappeared around each curve in the switchbacks. I'd wanted to be alone in that deep-woods quiet, and here were these happy humans. The higher we climbed, the farther their conversations carried through the thinning foliage. I failed to overtake the first pair and couldn't stay still long enough for the second to pass me. With each step, I rolled my eyes.

My stock memory of doing cocaine in North Carolina may not actually take place within the state lines: I am in the back seat of a black, soft top '88 Mustang. The story goes that its previous owner committed suicide (not necessarily in the car itself—though it was never said that *wasn't* the case). Its entire inside is spray-painted matte black. It is night, and the autumn air sneaks through the gaps between the roof and the car's metal body. I curl up underneath my boyfriend's felt coat, and I want so badly either to be asleep or to be alone.

The forward motion of the car isn't enough to calm my soul's jangling. We arrive home as the sun sneaks over the horizon, my body suspended between physical alertness and mental exhaustion like an animal in amber.

The switchback trail becomes a rock scramble at mile three. Doesn't that sound lovely? Like a type of breakfast. Blue blazes, spray-painted arrows, point the way forward.

I've heard clean people say, *I lost the power of choice.* I didn't understand that for a long time. I thought I was just shifting topography, always changing my mind—I couldn't say why.

I've also heard clean people say an *emotional bottom* occurs when circumstances fall faster than we can lower our expectations. For example: failing out of school, moving home, losing a job, being diagnosed with bipolar I, and being left by a boyfriend for a woman who prefers heroin. In clean-jargon, an emotional bottom is a time for change—either asking for help or getting decidedly worse.

Up on the rock scramble, the other hikers disappeared into crevices and around boulders. Alone at last. Granite stretched impressively and then sheered away into valley views. The trail markers were elusive, but I recognized sights from two years before. One tree in particular, its thick branches silver and bare, reassured me, *This is the way.*

A lie I told myself: I did not do any cocaine during the month I holed up, unemployed, in a pink bedroom with unregistered guns in the closet, so that meant I was getting better.

I couldn't have chosen when I would be done with the drugs because my choice was always more, whenever possible. I once snorted something (I don't know what) that burned so badly I hit myself in the face with the heel of my hand to feel something different.

I am convinced to this day that it is mostly the dying who move to Florida. In rehab, the nurses fed me pills upon pills upon pills—one for sleep, one for mood, one for my belly, another for sleep, another for mood, another for sleep. I skipped across the maroon carpet and passed out belly-up on the sidewalk where we patients smoked cigarettes.

We were allowed out as a group one night, and I stuck quarters into a jukebox to play "Casey Jones." I sang deep and low like I meant it, breathing into the bottom of my lungs, grinning. Everyone else was at least ten years older than me, and they collectively rolled their eyes, except for my roommate, who ran outside to smoke a cigarette saying something like it (like I) was too much.

The spindly tree did not point the way. Not the right one anyway. I followed false trail after false trail, dead-ending again and again at cliffs. The views were literally breathtaking. I could no longer hear the people who'd irritated me on the way up through the woods, and I started to become afraid.

After doing drugs for long enough, overdoses become notable only when resulting in death; the cliff face crumbles from natural erosion, exposure. Though loss of life might seem like a warning sign, it's often an excuse to get fucked up again, something else needing to be forgotten.

•

I lived in a halfway house with a woman who said she'd taught local dealers The Secret to cooking crack. It was my idea for us, each a month clean, to drive down to the south side. I should have gone alone but wanted company in my misery. She left me sitting outside a house with a bedsheet for its front door. She said, *Don't lock the car.* I breathed shallow until she returned with a small plastic bag, full. I would like to forget about this now that I've written it, but I think it is important that I remember.

A true thing no one believed: I did not steal my dad's sleeping pills when he came to visit.

There are different kinds of fear. Slick palms on a mile-long stretch of boulders are less than ideal. Part of the trail requires crawling across a rock only five feet wide, with a sheer rock face to the left and a hundred-foot drop to the right. I envisioned white bone cracking through skin looking like the beautiful tree that had led me astray. Fear is an ouroboros; it feeds itself.

The cocaine in Florida was unremarkable, and yet every memory I have from that time is distinct and jagged like the broken glass of a jar candle I threw against the halfway house's kitchen wall—even the pieces that looked smooth and easily handled were surprisingly sharp.

It's complicated even in medicine to parse truth from fiction, or diagnosis from diagnosis. Every junkie I know has been labeled, at least once, with a sickness other than addiction. Similarly, for people with bipolar I, the comorbidity rate for a substance use disorder is higher than fifty percent.

The doctors in rehab agreed with my diagnosis, even knowing about the cocaine. I learned my roommates' last names from orange bottles lined up on our shared nightstands. My tongue stretched around new words: *Abilify*, *Trazodone*, *Depakote*, *Seroquel*, *Lamictal*. Side effects include memory loss, confusion, disorientation.

After some time, I found the couples whom I'd been wishing away. They were bottlenecked at a crevasse that demanded a hiker jump from one ledge to another, some five feet below.

Hello! I said.

A man much taller than me climbed down, his legs spanning the distance, and then offered me his hand. My palms were wet and raw from pulling my body over boulders, but I didn't think to wipe them dry.

Thank you, I said.

Our fingers curled around one another's, and he took my weight.

I can't remember the last time I did cocaine, though it seems like I should. Most of the big endings in life pass without our knowing it in the moment. What we would have done differently!

•

One afternoon, the woman who'd left me sitting in her car cut a blue line on the kitchen table and said, *Try this.* The trail of powder was no longer than the nail on my pinkie I was insulted by its size, but she told me to trust her in a voice I'd never heard her use before. I handed over my body the same way a person prepares, willingly, to fall from a great height.

Sometimes what looks like a bottom drops out, and a person finds herself crawling along cool white floor tiles with bloodstains in the grout toward *more.*

I separated from the couples after the rock scramble and the cliffs. The trail down from the summit is flat and easy, more a walk than a hike but for its distance. At home, my hands peeling away from themselves, I admitted out loud that I should not have gone alone.

After I cleaned up and went back to college, a friend of mine declared in a literature course how *expected* and *overdone* he found stories about drugs. I nodded along emphatically. What I lacked in self-awareness I made up for with the earnest desire to pretend like the person I once was never existed.

What is this thing inside that demands we swallow ourselves? I want so badly to understand this behavior, to find a skeleton key that halts the complex series of gears and winches moving toward the obliteration of the self.

After graduation, I got tattooed in a half-abandoned strip mall. On the inside of my left arm is the final line from a story in *Jesus' Son*. The narrator, Fuckhead, seizes on the floor, hallucinating wet and green, a verdant landscape: "And you, you ridiculous people, you expect me to help you." Its final word and punctuation dip into my elbow ditch.

People who read the tattoo are often taken aback, like it's an affront, like they are the ridiculous ones. I've never said this outright, but here we are.

I've returned to the mountain again. See the cliff. Give me your hand.

inheritance

I

My favorite family photo was taken the evening of my parents' 32nd anniversary. The image breaks precedent: I am seated between my mother and father, instead of to one side. Positioned in this way, it's clear how much I look like them. My face could be a computer-generated composite of theirs, albeit one pushed backward in time.

This is the extent of my immediate family: my father, me, my mother. Growing up, we spent most holidays with friends instead of relatives. This was mainly a function of geography. My extended family is large and sprawling in a way particular to the recently immigrated. My mother's brothers live in Malaysia and Australia, and my father's cousins live in the western parts of Ukraine. In these countries I have relatives upon relatives, some of whom are close family friends but still addressed as Uncle and Auntie. When we visit, I am briefed: This person is married to that person who is this person's brother / cousin / aunt; these people were friends and then he married his friend's sister. Reunions only happen every so often and then, en masse.

After so many years together, my parents remain the only interracial couple in both their families. To my knowledge, this extends to my generation and the one after me as well. I am the odd-looking cousin. When we visit my father's family, they exclaim that I look like my mother; when we visit my mother's family, they say I take after my father. This is not to say my family has not claimed me, but rather that I have always felt out of place where I believed I should belong. It has been difficult for me to differentiate between what was passed down through blood and double helixes and what was if not unique then at least distinct to me as a person, rising from the conditions of my life.

Susan Sontag wrote that photographs "help people to take possession of a space in which they are insecure." I would argue that writing an essay does the same thing. Looking at the photograph above, I divide my face into pieces. I have my mother's coloring, nose (she semi-affectionately calls it the Mah-nose, passed down through her father's side), showing-teeth smile, and asymmetrical eyelids (these are from her mother). My father's features are fewer and more scattered across my face. I see its mirrored shape; his dimple, doubled and exaggerated in my cheeks; and the deep set of our eyes. But this is only the physical parsing—this is the easy part.

II

The exact cause of bipolar disorder is unknown. Researchers have identified haywire neurotransmitters like dopamine as playing an important role in mood turbulence as well as a vague genetic component. Bipolar disorder isn't necessarily hereditary, but it often runs in families. The most recent edition of the American Psychiatric Association's *Diagnostic and Statistical Manual of Mental Disorders* (the *DSM-5*) reports that family history "is one of the strongest and most consistent risk factors for bipolar disorders," though it's uncertain whether the reasoning for this falls down on the nature or nurture side of the age-old debate. Regardless, the likelihood of someone who has a family member with bipolar disorder having it themselves is ten times higher than someone with no family history.

Perhaps because of these uncertainties, the tools for diagnosing bipolar disorder and other mental illnesses are less empirical than those for sicknesses rooted below the brain. Family history is one such example. Doctors and counselors rely on the symptoms and diagnoses of a patient's relatives to identify and treat the patient's own illnesses. This information arrives through reporting and/ or medical records. Checks and balances—receiving stories from multiple sources allows a diagnosing physician to compare and contrast realities and memories. This helps to root out delusion, fear, resentment, all those base drives that lead to untruth, intentional or otherwise. In an ideal circumstance, at least two of the three sources (patient, family, or medical records) will point toward an agreed-upon past. But even this is troubling. How much can we really know of another person—especially those who are closest to us? I suspect more and more each year that we are made of some parts only visible to others and some parts only visible to ourselves. Put a group of humans in close proximity to one another and keep them there for generations, and they'll need to settle on a single public narrative that no one fully believes to keep the peace.

III

My mother told me in passing that her own mother was depressed, no details. I've only met this grandmother twice, both times before I turned fifteen. In my memories, she is the smell of joss sticks, a thin polyester fabric of purple flowers on a brown background, and an admonishment not to touch other people's faces. I cannot hear her voice. She may never have spoken to me directly; the scolding about my wayward hands was translated and relayed through my mother.

The rough sketches of my grandmother's life as I know them: She lived and died in a country over ten thousand miles away from where I am now. My grandmother never learned to drive, and her own mother could not walk properly, her feet bound into mincing golden lilies. My grandmother did not speak to her only daughter for almost a decade because my mother left home for America with an *orang puteh*. There's not much information there. Names are rearranged in Chinese so that the concept of "first name" doesn't translate verbatim—what I'm circling here is that I don't know my own grandmother's name.

After my grandmother died, my mother returned from the funeral across the ocean with gold jewelry and a small black-and-white photograph, its bottom right corner torn off. My grandmother stands to the right of her cousin, posed in front of a painted backdrop, their arms around each other's shoulders. Her beauty surprised me. She was thin, elfin, long-necked. I keep the photograph above my desk. Sontag writes that displaying a photograph in this fashion expresses "a feeling both sentimental and implicitly magical." I am laying "claim to another reality." In this imagined world, our connection is something of substance.

I don't mind, in this instance, the traditionally negative associations with sentimentality and unearned emotions.

Aesthetics be damned. Now that I have the photograph, I can see my face in hers. The piece of paper is only an image—a representation of reality instead of the thing itself—but what a compelling image. Her mouth, my mouth. Full and round in its bottom lip, this feature skipped my mother's generation. I see my hands in hers, too, unlovely, functional, looking like they belong to someone taller. Whatever else I've inherited remains a mystery to me.

IV

It is difficult for the mind to imagine beyond what is already known. Holy people and doctors served similar functions for most of humankind's years upon the planet and still do, in many places. A fact is true until it is disproven—the heretics who believed the Earth orbited the sun were tortured, burned, or banished; the women who insisted that their organs did not wander around their body were locked away. Some cultures and religions hold that sickness is both a spiritual and physical concern. Others believe it a question of moral character, specifically a lack thereof. Abstractions like willpower, reverence for the ancestors, courage, and cleanliness of the soul are all relevant factors when it comes to illness.

Mary Karr writes in *The Art of Memoir* that "we've lost faith in old authorities," in objectivity. Science is no longer an "unassailable [fount] of truth." As medicine changes, so does our understanding of disease and affliction. In light of new information, we must go around trying to identify past shapes we can only make out by their sepia-toned outlines. Great big perhapses become recorded into present-day medical records. No wonder we get it wrong sometimes.

V

My father's mother cycled between cackling, mischievous laughter; loud complaints I could not translate but understood through tone and volume; and morose tears. She made blueberry moonshine in mason jars, knitted blanket after blanket after blanket, grew tomatoes and spiny cucumbers and roses in the backyard, shoveled snow, canned fruits, and ensured an icon of the Virgin Mary looked down from a corner of each room in her red brick house. She reminded me of a Midwestern spring—surprisingly gentle and then cold and storming. The first phrase I learned in her native language was by osmosis: *I know, Mom.*

I don't think I look like my grandmother. Not even a little bit. A family photograph shows my father, his sister, my grandmother, and me at age three-ish. Here is our attempt at "bear[ing] witness to its connectedness." Sontag doesn't address what happens when the attempts fail. I sent the photo to my friend. *I look adopted*, I complained, half-joking. My friend laughed, presumably because I do.

When my grandmother died, I traveled north for her funeral. It was April and freezing. A wreath of white lilies hung from the front door's brass-colored knocker. No one but strangers entered the house that way. There was the funeral itself, the wake, and the burial. At the Catholic church she attended weekly, my grandmother's body was laid out in a pastel pantsuit, a string of pearls the color of her hair rested around her neck. Her parishioner friends, their heads covered with floral-print scarves, their coats bulky and dark, clustered in the alcoves and pews like a flock of so many pigeons worrying over a piece of bread. I overheard one woman speaking with another.

"She had a granddaughter," she said. "I know she did, but I don't see her here."

There I was, a few feet away, wearing all black, the only woman under fifty in the entire church, but unimaginable as the family in question. I take after my grandmother in less obvious ways: a laugh that startles with its sudden volume, an energy that keeps me in motion, an eye that seeks improvement and an inability to keep those observations to myself.

VI

Families keep secrets. Though from the outside it seems unreasonable not to disclose information when the health of a loved one is at stake, we are not always a reasonable species. From a less calculated perspective, secrets can be deemed simply irrelevant. In either case, a whisper can become a crack that widens far enough for a human to fall through.

I spent a semester abroad in college, and my father visited me that winter. We walked downtown and looked at monuments and caught up on one another's lives: my school, his work. That evening he surprised my mother with a phone call from both of us. As the line rang, he clicked the speaker button and put his finger to his lips.

"Hi," he said.

My mother answered with a statement. "Your sister called about your mother again. She's still in the hospital."

My father said nothing, blinked a few times. He looked at me, then at the phone.

"Hello?" she asked.

"Hi, yes, I'm here with Alysia," he answered.

No one spoke for at least ten seconds.

"I'll call my sister later," my father finally said.

Then we talked about our dinner plans.

After hanging up the phone, my father looked at me. He sighed. "Your grandmother," he said, "had a stroke."

"Is she okay? When did this happen?" I asked.

"She's alive. About a month ago."

Over dinner that night, he told me a story: When my grandmother was a teenager she'd seen her own father beaten by soldiers in the family garden and then die from his injuries. This was before the labor camps in Germany during the Second World War. Before she came over the Atlantic in a slow boat to America.

After the stroke, she never regained her speech and died a few months later. It took me too many years to learn that if I'd had her life, I would have acted exactly as she did, too.

When asked at the hospital, and then later at the rehab facility, if I had a family history of either mental illness or substance abuse, I said, *Yes*, to both. I used words like *depression* and *bipolar* and *alcoholism*. I told them my family did not go to doctors, but the way they behaved suggested to me that if they had, this is what professionals would have said. I believed that story wholeheartedly. I suspect now that it is incomplete.

It's tempting to insist upon causality. I want answers—if not why, at least how. I once asked a therapist, jokingly (we were always joking, she and I, which is why she was my favorite) if I could blame my family for everything wrong with me. *Everything* as in diagnoses, drug abuse, eating, psych ward, sad partners, self-harm.

She took a serious turn on me. I could tell by the way she moved her shoulders, and I curled up further into the small green armchair in anticipation of The Therapy.

"You could, but what good would that do? You still have to fix it."

I studied the small cut-glass bowls of M&Ms and Skittles on the table between us. I could feel her looking at me.

She kept talking. "I've never met a parent—even the ones who beat the shit out of their kids—who thought they were not doing what was best for their child."

"My parents didn't do that," I said.

"It was an example."

When children are children, it is difficult to imagine the hurt they will cause when they grow up. Eula Biss writes, "some apologies are unspeakable. Like the one we owe our parents." We remember life differently, my parents and I.

Especially my father and I. This disagreement, at least, we can agree upon. We each believe we are long-suffering of the other's behavior. Poor us, what did we do to deserve such a father, such a daughter?

A snapshot of me as a baby shows my face already pursed like a worried dog's. I am sitting on the walkway of a small pedestrian bridge, looking between the carved railings. When I showed it to a friend, he noticed something else.

"What is that knee?" he asked.

I looked and considered. On the left side of the photo is an adult's leg. Their body is cut out of the frame, but it's clear they are standing just close enough that I am easily within arm's reach. "I think it's my father's," I answered.

Now that years have passed since I lived at home I can say this: I think it is my father's because he would not have left me alone to fall.

Sontag cautions that "photography makes us feel that the world is more available than it really is." Available as in accessible, knowable. To trace our wounds back to a single place of origin—wouldn't this be ideal? Look back to my parents' parents, and then their parents, and so on. A single seed, deep below ground, blooming into this life: a rosebush, many headed, fragrant, difficult to handle, but able to survive the inevitable long periods of frost. There, see how the small, new leaves are miniatures of the ones already fallen on the ground?

deep-sea creatures

We are at a spiritual retreat in a Florida state park in January, and it is below freezing outside. Inside, the heating vents are loud, so loud we are nearly shouting to be heard. Cigarette smoke fills the upper third of the large room. This is the last habit we kick.

The retreat is for addicts. It allows for celebration of time away from vices, for discussion of how they remain. Most attendees suffer from some type of substance abuse: cheap liquor thrown up first thing in the morning, lighter burns on finger edges, track marks in the armslegsfeet. Once the substances are gone, other problems linger. We make wishes on lottery tickets and card hands. We struggle to leave abusive partners. We watch pornography compulsively. We tear open our bodies with sharp objects.

The retreat feels cult-like, theoretically nondenominational but interspersed with prayers and hymns that make reference to unending mercy, and this nagging impression is exacerbated by the knowledge that there are similar weekend pilgrimages held across the United States. People travel hours to attend, and it is common to see familiar faces, *old-timers*, at the retreats scattered throughout the southeastern states: in woodsy cabins on the outskirts of Gainesville; next to a decrepit barbecue shack in Brooksville, Florida; on the shores of Lake Allatoona, an hour north of Atlanta. The location is the most defining part of the experience; the rest blurs together in three nights of sleep deprivation, too much caffeine and nicotine, and familiar faces talking about similar pains.

Our second night in the woods, we sit and listen. A familiar man stands at the front of the smoke-heavy room. He thanks everyone for his presence at this retreat, for his general continued existence. He is grateful for their love. It makes all things possible. He talks about his struggles, about how he drove past the Hard Rock Casino on I-4 to get to this weekend. He says he wanted to pull over. And what's more, he dislikes his body, has now switched one habit of excess for another.

"I'm fucking fat," he says. "I hate myself. How I look. But here I—"

He turns in my direction.

I don't notice at first. But then he says my name—*and I hope she doesn't mind me saying this*—and I know what will come next.

The crowd is now watching me, not him, and I look up and meet his eyes to avoid everyone else's. What happens next is inevitable.

He says I am beautiful, keeps repeating the word. He says when I took off my shirt to go swimming when he met me so many years ago, he was struck by the contrast of me—*beautiful*—and my scars, thin and raised and white, running down my right arm and up both my sides. *Beautiful.* I am torn between resting on its three syllables of praise like a crutch and rejecting it for its superficiality.

He says my lack of self-consciousness, my beauty despite

the scars, as if they could somehow be separated from my body, inspires him to hate his own figure less. His eyes fill with grateful, loving tears. I smile and nod. I am gracious. But I do not feel empowered or empowering. I am resentful.

This man brings attention to parts of my body and life I'd rather ignore. I become self-conscious, and the feeling lingers. The next time I go swimming in public, nine months later, I think about my sides, about wrapping my arms around myself and resting a hand above each hipbone. I feel echoes of teenage embarrassment, a familiar desire to disappear. I do not want anyone to see my body and think about its contrasts, to be inspired in any way by its raised lines.

The authors of the *DSM-5* have finally suggested that self-harm is not necessarily linked to suicidal desires or an indicator of another illness. Until this most recent edition, published in 2013, nonsuicidal self-injury (NSSI) was written in as a symptom of borderline personality disorder—the cliché example is Glenn Close in the film *Fatal Attraction*. Think delusional, obsessive, wound so tightly that violence seems inevitable.

The behaviors, personalities, and interpersonal relationships of people with pure borderline personality disorder are often very different from those with NSSI. We in the latter category are a much more docile bunch. Furthermore, different neurotransmitters, though all likely haywire, fire in the brain when individuals with borderline and individuals with NSSI injure their bodies.

Despite its recent separation from borderline personality disorder, NSSI still does not stand alone. The *DSM-5* authors "found that most individuals with nonsuicidal self-injury have symptoms that also meet criteria for other diagnoses," particularly eating and substance abuse disorders. That last bit is reiterated toward the end of the entry; the authors bring up a 2012 study "that found that nonsuicidal self-injury is a predictor of substance use/misuse." For further details, see: uncomfortable retreats in remote locations.

My most visible scars are on the lateral side of my right arm. They draw stares. There is a small group clustered around my shoulder and tracks of them spaced almost evenly from one inch above my elbow to two inches above my wrist. I made them in two spurts, a few months apart.

The shoulder was first. It was a new place on my body, somewhere I hadn't yet broken in. The line down my arm I made another day, all in one go. I stood in the common room of a shared apartment, alone, my bare feet cool on the white tile floor. I don't remember why I did it, and I only briefly reflected on the soon-to-be-wounds' visibility and the likelihood of staining the grout. I couldn't stop once I started. I was frustrated by the absence of pain, the absence of blood. I sliced and sliced—compulsive, frantic, rabid.

These scars are sometimes mistaken for a type of adornment. I think this is because of their prominent location, their even pattern. Body modification has an old history, and intentionally scarring the flesh has been used to denote rites of passage—a woman may mark her stomach to indicate the onset of menstruation—or as a type of permanent ornamentation—there's that word *beautiful* again—for centuries. Altering the skin moves a person from one social group to another. Depending on the context, this movement can be positive, but it also can be ostracizing; the body is a battleground of belonging.

One summer, I spent what felt like two weeks straight in a print shop, setting type, throwing my shoulder behind a Vandercook drum cylinder, binding books, making and marbling paper. I wore baggy, short-sleeved t-shirts because of the heat and the oil and the small metal shavings that left black smudges across fabric. The people I met and worked with during that time became close because of the long hours and small spaces, our unfamiliarity with heavy, hot metals and specialized equipment bonding us.

One woman, who specialized in sculpture and paper-making, had recently returned from Tanzania, where she'd studied traditional manufacturing techniques and design. I admired her, sat next to her while we worked, watched her fleshy, capable hands run a bone folder down the spine of a book with confidence and just the right amount of pressure. She looked at me, her gaze strong and direct, while I sat on a metal folding chair, hunched over my spread legs, elbows on knees.

"Scarification," she said.

I was confused.

She pointed to my arm. "Nice."

I may have said, *Thank you*. I likely said, *Thank you*. She was assuming the best of me.

I am eighteen when I arrive at my first retreat. There are fresh cuts on my sides, and the first aid supplies under the communal kitchen counter are insufficient to deal with the stickiness and heat of the skin around my wounds. No one here mistakes my cuts for anything but what they are, and the gossip—a trip off property for gauze and antiseptic—travels fast, propelled by a pervasive sense of righteousness and a desire to help. And so it is here, in the almost-countryside of Brooksville, Florida, near a barbecue shack that prominently displays a glass jar full of nails labeled "Obama Sauce," where I meet adults who cut themselves.

The first is a woman who wraps herself in scarves and bells; practices reiki; and dances, ecstatic and wild, at the weekly drum circles on her local beach. She is maybe forty, maybe fifty, seems kind and fierce. I remember nothing of what she says to me the night I meet her, only that she holds my gaze and says things that sound capital-t True, which is to say, if they are not universal truths, they at least resonate deep within both of us. I wish to become fussed over and a favorite of hers, a surrogate child of sorts, but our relationship is brief. She wants only to let me know it is not necessary to hurt myself in the way that I do.

The second is a man who, despite his youthful demeanor and face, is bald and walks with a cane. I guess he favors his legs for abuse because I know he still cuts himself and his arms are free of scabs. I wonder if he is responsible for his limp. This is probably untrue, but I will not understand the myriad of ways a middle-aged body can fail for many more years. His cane is thick, a shiny silver knob at its top, and I will remember this about him best of all. This and the way he introduces himself: *Hi, my name is Art, and I'm a cutter.* His candor surprises.

He tells me something very different from the belled woman. His self-injury is the least of his evils; he struggles with depression and, despite years sober, still craves alcohol in suicidal quantities. He tells me not to be ashamed. I sit on the floor of the large meeting room, hugging my knees, a wallpaper of faded daffodils behind me. Art sits in a white plastic chair, and I am nearly eye level with his cane's knob. He looks down at me and says that should it ever come down to it, should I ever be placed in a position where I feel so trapped, trapped in the ways that he still feels, I should pick up the razor blade.

To meet the criteria for NSSI, a person must intentionally injure herself at least five days out of a calendar year without suicidal intentions. Relatively socially appropriate behaviors like body piercings, tattooing, nail-biting, and scab-picking do not count toward the allotted five incidents. Neither does scarification, though the lasting results can look remarkably similar. What separates flesh-tearing body modification from the disorder is the motivation behind the act, which, for NSSI, is generally as follows:

— To obtain relief from a negative feeling or cognitive state.

— To resolve an interpersonal difficulty.

— To induce a positive feeling state.

The *DSM-5* authors also note that to individuals with NSSI, self-injury provides near immediate relief and, more troubling, the act of harming eventually becomes necessary for respite. At least, that's how it feels.

We train our brains, create neural pathways that work like ruts in a well-traveled road. Research suggests that self-injury is often concurrent with drug abuse and that pain itself can be addictive. Pavlov is famous for his bell causing salivation, and it's almost funny, watching a dog's large, pleading eyes and droplets of saliva dripping out the sides of its mouth, but our brains are wired just like that damn dog's: stimulus, response. The difference between us and the dog is that we often train ourselves.

I have now spent more of my life not ruining my body than I have mutilating it. But the urge remains. It rears it head, snarling, at times of intense unpleasant emotions. My brain says that if I tear my flesh, the hurt inside will stop, will mutate into a form I can salve. It does not think about consequences; it is incapable of conceptualizing the future tense.

What happened to your arm? strangers ask. Maybe once for every five times, the question is posed with what appears to be genuine concern, with wide-open eyes. Some people have no idea that self-harm exists, and my best guess is that they fear I've been in some awful accident.

The other four times, I want to hurt the people who ask. I want to hurt them badly. With their question, their faces twist into an almost-smirk or a wry, judging appraisal.

I am an imperfect person. I have considered making up elaborate stories about kidnapping and torture, about detonating bombs and rogue explosions, about traumatic car accidents and arms through windshields. What these stories have in common, of course, is that I am not the subject in the story who is responsible for the damage. I am the object, the body that is acted upon.

The Truths that exist and are shared between people who have intentionally injured themselves are like boneless deep-sea creatures that do not belong in sunlight, among normal conversation, without thousands of pounds of pressure holding them together. Here is one: The deep cuts don't bleed at first. After the skin opens, there is a pause. Maybe half a second. The white lining of fat underneath the outer two layers of skin is visible. Then blood. The longer the pause, the more the cut bleeds.

I wonder if truth-telling would be the best way to hurt those people who've asked me smirking questions.

Occasionally, the questions are necessary. I do not count these as questions-asked-by-strangers because it is the job of medical professionals to ensure their patients are mentally sound and free of suffering. But despite my best efforts, I find myself still bothered at times. More recently a new doctor lightly dragged a pointer finger down my arm.

"What is this?" she asked.

"Exactly what it looks like," I said.

The retreat on Lake Allatoona's shore is held in April, when the southern flora is in full bloom, and October, when the air is crisp and breathable. The food is the best here because the person who does the cooking is a chef. He and his one-armed girlfriend dice and mince and sauté and steam and pluck and debone for hours on Friday and Saturday afternoons. For reasons I never figure out—they are picky and fastidious about whom they allow to help with tasks—they accept me into the kitchen. So while at the other retreats I walk around like a raw nerve, here in Georgia I settle into the steam of the kitchen and feel at peace.

A group of men from a halfway house comes up for the weekend. One of them has a baby face and sweet drawl, and he works with me in the kitchen. Whether this comes from a desire to take time away from the men he lives with, my continued presence, or an aversion to taking off his shirt while playing volleyball, I'm not sure. We spend large chunks of the weekend side by side, our backs to the stove, looking out into the meeting room through a large opening cut out of a wall and used to serve food. Framed in such a way, I'm sure we look happy and content.

I push my sleeves above my elbows while cutting vegetables. Though I'd normally keep them down to cover my scars, it's not worth the fabric dragging pieces of food up my arms. I rock a knife back and forth over so many cloves of peeled garlic, unencumbered. My companion, however, is struggling. Every minute or so he pauses to pull down his sleeves as they ride up past his wrists, catching small bits of onion in the process.

When he finally caves to convenience and folds up the fabric, I see fresh cuts on the fleshy part of his inner forearm. I do not say anything. We work in silence until an old-timer comes in.

"Good lord, boy, who gave you a knife?" he asks.

My companion stutters and turns a bright, bright red.

I think of Art with his silver cane and direction to be unashamed. My companion is nearly a decade older than me, but I feel responsible for passing on what I've learned in my year of retreats. I will assure him later that the man is only teasing, that the man is no stranger to pain, that this retreat is a wild place where those deep-sea secrets are brought into the light and examined, poked, sometimes even tickled.

And it is also in this sort of place I will learn, in the coming years, when a man stands at the front of a room and calls me beautiful, that sometimes these creatures bite, that it is in their natures to attack when provoked, even if for the best of reasons.

Tearing open the body is contagious. This is also identified in the *DSM-5*, that "recommendation or observation of another" is how individuals often discover the behavior. It's as if the capacity or desire for self-destruction is innate but the methods for how an individual chooses to do so are learned. More distressingly, studies conducted in the '80s found that if a person who self-injures is brought into an inpatient treatment unit, the behavior can spread like an infection disseminated by sight.

And though this is how it begins, it is harder to determine why it does. The baffling question: Why would someone think self-injury is a good idea? The *DSM-5*'s attempts to answer it are vague and broad. The authors suggest cutting could be a form of punishment, an act of penance or redemption. I do not know if there is a clinical term for the desperate search to alleviate the force of a feeling.

What happens next is easier to explain. Once an individual starts to cut or self-harm, the neural pathways form. As the brain associates emotional relief with physical pain, negative or positive reinforcement take over, depending on the person and her motivations. These are the same withholding and reward systems used to train pets.

What is important, in the process of training a dog, is to reward the animal immediately after the correct action. What is equally important—perhaps more important— is to withhold the bone occasionally because inconsistent rewarding is the most compelling. So even if the injury does not provide emotional relief every time, the person is still hooked, maybe even more so. The lack of certainty drives the quest for relief ever forward.

I decided not to buy vitamin E or any other type of scar-healing cream after I stopped cutting. I was proud of the marks for a time, both during and immediately after. There was something about the translation of an emotional pain to a physical one that made me feel I was built of stronger stuff than the unmarked person next to me. Intentionally cutting one's body requires a special sort of determination—how an animal gnaws off a limb when caught in a trap. The action contradicts our inclination to avoid pain, injury, and infection.

In popular culture, the person who self-harms is portrayed one of two ways: mopey and languishing, staring forlornly at the arms, the thighs, the desired place of injury; or frantic and wild, like there is too much energy bundled into sinewy limbs. Of course, most people fall into neither of these groups. I like to think no one would suspect me if it weren't for my visible scars.

My friend's daughter has been asking what happened to my arm for six years now. I have alternately told her it was a cat, a car accident, and that I would explain when she is older. She has recently taken to claiming that she is, in fact, *older now*. And though she looks like a teenager, she is eleven and still ignorant of all the ways people can hurt themselves. I do not know what the appropriate age is to speak honestly about this or if I am the person to have the conversation with her. I am afraid. I do not want to be the one who makes her aware there are people who do this as a means of comfort, am terrified she might try it one day, regardless of whether or not I speak to her about it, using my body as inspiration for what to do to her own.

On the other hand, I worked, for a time, at a high school whose students came from the poorest parts of a dying industrial town, came from an F-rated middle school where half the honors program received failing grades. I was in charge, sometimes, of escorting students through the hallways—to their lockers, to the nurse's office, to the bathroom, to the principal's office—because they could not be trusted to arrive at their intended destination safely or at all. One of them, a thin blonde, elbowed me lightly in the ribs. I raised an eyebrow at her.

"You shouldn't do that." She pointed to my arm.

"I don't anymore. It was a long time ago."

I don't think she believed me.

"It's no fucking good," she said. "Cut it out."

My medical history is becoming a revisionist one.

Consider this: The information about NSSI is from a section at the very end of the *DSM-5* entitled "Conditions for Further Study." The chapter opens with a call for continuing research that "will allow the field to better understand these conditions and will inform decisions about possible placement in forthcoming editions." This disorder, if it ever exists, will not become official until many years after I have stopped ripping open my own skin.

The *DSM* does not deal with treatment for disorders, only with their identification, but consider then what it means that I have stopped, that the not-yet-a-disorder has been healed or cured without the recommended care, whatever it will be.

In Georgia, at the October retreats, we eat turkey on Saturday nights. It serves as an early Thanksgiving of sorts, and the next morning we sit on the porch overlooking the lake and pick through the carcass to make sandwiches. And so on a Sunday afternoon, as I pack to leave, the old-timer who'd walked into the kitchen and made the joke about the knife hands me the winning half of a wishbone.

"Here," he says.

I do not understand.

"My wish was that you wouldn't hurt yourself anymore. Keep this."

I am frustrated by his superstition, like his wish made on a dead animal's body could in some way help my living one. I want to say something hurtful. Instead, I take the bone home. I wrap it in string and hang it around my rearview mirror. Some people ask after it, what sort of gris-gris magic do I have there. I rarely answer, but the truth is that I cut myself a few days before that October retreat and have not done so since.

The bone hangs there for the next six years, surviving both an international and a cross-country move, before simply snapping in half of its own volition during a cold Midwestern winter. It's as if it stayed intact long enough for me not to worry that the bone was the only thing keeping my urges in check, long enough for me to retrain my brain to want different, to want better.

three men

This one was blond, this one brunette, this one that unwashed-looking in-between. He was tall. He was thin. He had brown eyes, blue eyes, green eyes. His face veered more toward beautiful than handsome, with a particular feature keeping it shy of perfection: a too-large nose, a cartoonish jawline, a weak chin. He was sad.

If it's difficult holding this chimera of features together, picture instead the lead singer of The Doors at his most iconic: shirtless, in fitted pants, clean-shaven, angular, slightly petulant, prone to wild elaborations. Consider me a fortunate woman. I'll bundle these men together and call them all Jim.

He was eighteen the first time he tried to commit suicide and hung himself from the ceiling fan in his bedroom. When Jim told me this story, years later, we were lying in bed. He rested on his side, head propped up on his hand instead of the pillow. I lay on my back, and the white plastic blades of a different fan spun above me. I played a game with myself: Pick a single blade and watch it complete its entire revolution again and again and again until what feels like the nerves rooting my eyes in their sockets hurt and I have to focus instead on something fixed, like the motor or the ceiling.

"I can't believe you thought it would hold your weight," I said.

"The cord snapped, not the fan."

"Really?" I asked.

"It was more a cry for help," he replied.

I watched the fan. I think he watched me watch it. Its movement was silent, but I imagined cartoon noises as my eyes moved circles in their sockets: *whomp, whomp, whomp.*

"I ate a pack of cigarettes before that," he said.

I snorted. "That was stupid."

"They're poisonous."

"What?" There was a bottle of liquid nicotine on his bookshelf in our living room.

"That bottle—" He pointed in a vague direction and answered the question I hadn't verbalized. "One or two sips could kill you."

"Oh," I said. "Is it quick?"

He raised his head off his hand, shook his head. "Slow. Painful."

"That's too bad."

That day, Jim's father had opened the bedroom door, seen the snapped cord hanging from the fan and cigarette butts covering the bed, and called an ambulance.

"The paramedic asked how much pain I was in on a scale of one to ten. 'Ten,' I answered." Jim laughed, but the bed beneath us stayed still. "I was such an angsty teenager. The medic looked at his partner—I guess he was training him or something—and said, 'This is what I have to deal with.'"

Jim spent that night in the ER, and the hospital admitted him for an involuntary 72-hour psychiatric hold.

•

I first met Jim in high school. Back then, he lived with his father in a big, dark house off a long winding road. His back yard opened up onto greenery, a large lawn with an odd bamboo grove bordered by oak trees. His dog, an old chocolate lab streaked silver in the face and named after one of the local waterways, kept him company most days. A white bottle of St. John's Wort, its label illustrated with the yellow blossoming herb, sat dusty on the kitchen counter. Jim's mother lived up North, alone but for the company of many cats. When they spoke on the phone she'd unload her sadness—her loneliness, her struggles to leave bed, her desire to disappear. It's not a surprise that Jim's wired the same way. A family history of depression is one of the illness' primary risk factors; sadness and self-destruction often run in the blood.

Jim slept erratically, taking long walks early in the morning and late at night around neighborhoods not designed for pedestrians while wearing headphones, his music turned up so loud he wouldn't have heard a car if it was headed right for him, horn blaring. This habit continued as an adult. When we were together, I was often alone in bed. The mattress' shifting to take or give up his weight eventually stopped waking me.

After weeks of this, he'd sleep for what seemed like days on end. Though he deserved rest, exhausted from his restless nights, the days and their obligations continued to revolve and pass him by as he remained immobile under the covers. When unconscious, he ground his teeth together so hard they squeaked, bone on bone. I wanted to squeeze his arms, burrow my face into the small hollow at the center of his chest and breathe my life into his. I also wanted to drag him out of bed, shouting. How quickly my compassion twists into something vicious when I am afraid.

I would like to say I understood Jim, but I've never really tried to kill myself. The undertone of my teenage years was more *this could be it* instead of *this is it*, conditional rather than definite. The most dangerous things I did were careless. Jim was different. His illness was pervasive and corrosive, not like a high pH acid but like time. It was different, too, because, as a rule, I tend to spiral up and out, rather than in and down—space flight versus deep-sea diving.

Even though I'd spent time with my own sickness, its effects had been limited to a few years. Either I was on the best psychiatric medication ever or—or something else. I didn't know what that something was then, but I sensed that Jim was different from me. Being with him was sometimes like standing in a glass-bottomed boat, watching another world carry on aslant, below. By the time we dated, I'd been living with a diagnosis of bipolar I for nearly seven years. I had been medicated for the same amount of time. Next to him, I felt strangely stable, solid in my own body while he was dissolving around the edges.

The second time Jim tried to kill himself was when he was half-grown, out of his father's house, living with a bunch of boys in a Southern state. He had been working as a delivery driver and showed up to his shift too drunk for his boss to pretend like it wasn't happening. Jim returned home, defeated, impulsive.

"My roommate's girlfriend had blister packets of Tylenol lying around. I drank a handle of Evan Williams—that's all I remember," Jim said.

We were sitting on our ugly blue couch for this conversation, our feet resting on our makeshift coffee table. I scrunched up my nose at the whiskey's specificity, though I knew Jim liked his liquor cheap and effective, had figured out the economics of cents to alcohol by volume, had run a moonshine still out of his bedroom.

"What happened?" I asked.

"I guess I told my roommate," he said.

"You guess?" I heard my voice lurch upward like a startled seagull. Listening to Jim's stories, I transformed into a fretful, hand-wringing woman from a Victorian novel. I'd forget all of my own *nearlys* and *almosts*, all the stupid close calls, and rather than feel lucky that either of us had made it this far into our lives, I'd worry that Jim might disappear any minute. He knew the best, that is, the quickest, ways to die. Tylenol overdose is not one of them. Instead, it results in slow liver failure, spending helpless days in a bed in excruciating pain, the end inevitable.

"My roommate said I was hilarious that night." Jim smiled and rubbed his bare feet together, tendons and veins flexing with the movement. "Like, I was the funniest I'd ever been. We were having a great time, and at some point I told him what I'd done. I don't remember this at all."

Jim's roommate drove him, speeding, to the hospital. A cop pulled them over and made them call an ambulance. His roommate waited for the ticket and sent Jim ahead in a series of flashing lights.

I understood the absence of memory. Jim and I had an intimacy built in part on empty spaces. He knew me, what the doctors had said about me, what I was afraid my mind could and would do of its own accord. We'd let one another in to see what was missing, shared our speculations about what lurked there in the murky waters.

As a teenager, Jim took all combinations of antidepressants and found them wanting. The pills hadn't helped his mother either, and so by the time we lived together, Jim distrusted all psychiatric medication. He didn't like psychologists either. This wasn't something he said, but something I noticed. Perhaps it's unfair to make that claim. I've met few straight men who will willingly talk about their feelings when not in crisis, and even fewer who will talk about them with anyone other than a woman they've slept with.

While we shared a house, Jim went to see a counselor. It's likely I suggested he talk to someone about his frequent desire to stay in our bedroom with the blinds shut, sleeping all day. After three sessions, he came home to say that the therapist had pronounced him no longer in need of her services.

A few nights later, after we'd argued in semi-reasonable tones about the state of our relationship and who *was* that woman he was spending so much time with and why *did* I feel the need to harp on small grievances like sponges in the sink, things were quiet. I had claimed the bed for my own sulking that night and lay on my back. The lights and fan were on, and I nursed my self-righteousness. *I fucking knew it*, I thought. *Whomp, whomp, whomp*, the fan replied.

Jim pushed open the cracked door. "I have to tell you something," he said.

What a line. The possibilities galaxied outward and then sucked back in to one sharp, unexpected point.

"I've been thinking about killing myself again," he said. "I've been thinking about it for a while now."

"I'm sorry," I said.

"Just thought you should know." And then he left the room, leaving the door wide open behind him. I heard him settle into the chair in front of his computer. It was just me and the fan again.

It is through our relationships with others that we best come to know ourselves. What is more than or less than without another body for comparison? Ideally, the more people we meet, the greater, the broader, our understanding of humanity becomes. Ideally, this makes us kinder.

I felt like I was floating. First out of bed, then into the next room where Jim sat. I'm sure the neighbors could hear. It was as if my lungs had lifted themselves out of my throat. We both needed some goddamn counseling. The next morning, I woke up hoarse, and Jim was still alive. His body, my body, our bodies out of control.

Toward the end of our romantic relationship, I had the impression we were both going selectively deaf. We came away from conversations remembering different versions of what was said. Our experiences of reality were splitting away from one another. After I'd said I was leaving, I asked if he was going to kill himself. That went over as well as I deserved, which is to say, badly.

We maintained a wary truce of friendship for a year. The problem was that we still fought like people who are afraid of how and to what extent the other can and will hurt them: claws unsheathed, defensive. Though we continued to act our worst, it was no longer accompanied by our best. He said I was cruel and mocking; I said he was a liar. We were both right sometimes.

It wasn't all bad, of course. These stories are some of the lowest of the lows in a long-term love. I remain and will remain grateful for his constancy, how he allowed me to see myself more clearly. Though he never suggested I stop taking my own psychiatric medication, his dislike of it meant he supported my decision to visit a doctor to see what would happen if I did. The violence he sought against his own body shone a light, showed the details and teeth, of the shadowy creatures I feared in myself. They were not what I thought they were. Jim taught me to be unafraid, to look and see.

Some friends of mine talk about stories in terms of beats, that every subplot has three of them, but this isn't fiction—thankfully, regretfully.

The third time Jim tried to kill himself, he meant it.

"It's the only time I'd obsessed about it for a while before," he said. "That time." He'd planned. He'd stocked up: Roxys, Xanax bars, another handle of whiskey. A rubber band and a plastic bag.

We were back in bed, lying supine. It was easiest for me not to look at him when we talked about these things. The fan spun above us.

"That should've killed you," I said.

"It should've," he agreed. "I woke up eighteen hours later with the plastic bag on my forehead and found the Xanax in the couch cushions."

The image was funny in the way that it presents a choice between hysterical laughter or tears—nothing in between is permissible. Perhaps this explains why Jim had a face that seemed always on the verge of a grin.

"You didn't pull it over your face?" I asked.

He shook his head. "I must've passed out before I got to that."

He pissed himself while he was out. His right foot was numb for the next six months.

How easy it is for us to die. How hard it is for us to actually end our lives.

Jim had trouble keeping a job before, while, and after we were together. Whether it was a three-year string of awful luck or him being the common difficult denominator in a series of workplaces is still unclear. Regardless, he'd had enough and decided to move far, far away. He'd been talking about overhauling his life for a long time—even while we were together. Our year of shitty friendship ended around the same time he scraped together savings, borrowed money from his mother and packed.

He announced his departure to me shortly before he moved, while we sat on the sloping, black driveway of his house, hunched over in bad postures. A pack of cigarettes, a lighter, and our cell phones lay around us like a magic spell.

"I'm leaving," he said.

I lit another cigarette after stubbing out another I'd only smoked down three-quarters. "To where?" I asked.

He pushed his hair back from his face with his hand splayed out. "Not sure yet. To my mom's first."

He'd told me a few months before this, in passing, that he'd again been thinking about killing himself, but didn't want to leave a mess behind for his roommates. "All my stuff. My body," he'd said. He hadn't mentioned it since, and I hadn't brought it up.

"Your mom's?" My implications hung in the summer humidity.

He shrugged.

"Then? After?"

He shrugged again.

Endings were on my mind. One of my best friends had died unexpectedly a month before this conversation, and I was in a storm of mourning I couldn't navigate. An urban legend says cats will eat the bodies of their dead owners, and I imagined awful cartoonish scenes of zombie violence. Perhaps grief is responsible for what happened next.

"If you decide to do anything—" I trailed off. I started again. I couldn't get it out. Then, in a rush: "If you decide to kill yourself or anything, will you let me know? A delayed email or something? I wouldn't, I don't—"

I found myself smiling in apology. I couldn't accept the responsibility of his life and wouldn't try to stop him, but wasn't able to let him go cleanly into whatever future he was choosing. I find it difficult, still, to care for people well. In my memory, he nodded like he understood, though this may be wishful absolution.

I want to have done better. In addition to providing part of the motivation to stop taking my pills, Jim saw me through the slow withdrawal process. To stop taking psychiatric medication after seven years is not an easy task. On my best days I was anxious and irritable. On my not-best, I was convinced that I'd accidentally drank poison or pulled over every ten minutes while driving to check my tire pressure because *I swear I felt something*. I owe debts of love and patience that I will be forever trying to repay.

We sat quietly in the driveway. Our postures worsened. I finished my cigarette. I told him I was happy that he was finally making the change he wanted, hugged him and left.

·

A friend once described their romantic relationships as fitting into the Jungian archetypal dynamic of the wounded healer—that is, they were trying to fix their partner's matching, more acute injuries. Consistently self-centered, I wondered at the time if they were trying to comment on my own behaviors. If so, they were close. I think I like sad men because though our hurts are similar, we are all foils in our clumsy attempts to outrun them. Where I tornadoed, Jim was motionless; where I attacked, he withdrew. A graceless attempt at balance.

I have had neither a manic nor a depressive episode in the four years since weaning off my psychiatric medication, confirming that my bipolar I was misdiagnosed. But the best part of this story is that Jim is still alive. Time and distance have salvaged some semblance of us.

The last time I saw Jim was a year after we'd sat in his driveway and talked about him dying. He smelled the same, was loping and pleasant, and smiled like he was happy to see me. I borrowed a pair of his shorts, and we went to the beach with my friends. He flirted with one, would kiss her in the coming days. The trip to the seaside was long and hot, but the cold, dark Atlantic felt like air in our lungs. We shrieked like children when diving under. In the sun, I browned and he burned across his chest where he put on sunscreen haphazardly, pink showing up with finger-streaks of white as the sun set. I chattered too much before we settled once again into one another's company, able to be friends again, in love with other people. Late at night, in my airconditionless apartment, we exchanged new confidences, soothed by the white noise whir of so many harmless, spinning fans.

withdrawal

BEFORE

very obviously strange structure

3rd person perspective

Following diagnosis of bipolar I, subsequent medication management, and behavioral therapy, Patient has stopped using cocaine. She is paid to make coffee. She is paid to sell bad Italian food. She stops seeing the world vibrate.

Patient claims she has matured (is no longer a reckless, feral girl-child bent on obliteration of the self) and suggests she might stop taking her sleeping medication. When she does not take her pill at the same time every night, she claims to experience a sensation similar to opiate withdrawal. We eliminate the medication.

Sleeping pill elimination successful. Average time Patient lies awake each night starting at the Absolut Vodka ads taped to her studio walls: 75 minutes.

Patient requests a decrease in her mood stabilizer. She is even less feral now and has enrolled in one community college course (Introduction to Mass Media Communications). She says, *Maybe I am not, in fact, ill.* The ends of all her sentences curve upward into questions. We reduce her medication with a warning: bipolar I is a lifetime diagnosis, though we concede that perhaps Patient could do with a smaller dosage.

Second opinions are legitimate requests, but Patient feels like she is being unfaithful (guilt). We know anyway; we see everything. The appointment's results are inconclusive. We provide no answers, but instead ask rhetorical questions and smile like a cat with a dish of milk. Our bookshelves are full of texts as thick as her palm is wide. Patient is uneasy and returns to us in our original form. She accepts the original diagnosis and subsequent course of treatment.

First dosage decrease is unremarkable. We asked Patient to disclose her medication changes to two people who will monitor her behavior (bipolar I patients ~~cannot be trusted~~ are notoriously resistant to taking medication), and both they and the Patient agree she has remained stable thus far. We are surprised. We decrease the dosage again.

Patient's boyfriend, one of the checks she has put in place, suggests she stop *fiddling* with her medication and claims Patient is acting *differently*. He says Patient is irritable; she snaps where before she smiled. Privately, Patient knows her upturned mouth is directed elsewhere—she smiles too broadly at a tall co-worker who is more convenient than handsome, whom she brushes past while carrying so many glasses on a small, circular tray. Dutiful, Patient tells us, and we tweak her dosage back up.

5 YEARS PASS

Patient moves out of state. Before leaving, she is discharged from our care and told she can now see a general practitioner for her monthly bottle of pills. We are all smiles. Patient is all smiles. Patient is now no longer a patient. Her illness is *well-managed*.

Living in a house on an acre of land with wild corn growing in the yard, Patient enrolls in graduate school. She becomes increasingly distressed, exhausted, and restless and despondent by turns. Distorted perceptions and erratic moods reoccur. Patient worries, quietly, that these are warning signs of a return to the psych ward. The worries build and culminate in what should be a minor, forgettable incident—a bicycle helmet clipped too tightly under her chin—that instead triggers what Patient's friends describe as a *flashback* (Patient herself denies this word choice). Wanting to preserve agency and autonomy, Patient makes an appointment at a local counseling center, not for medication management, but for talk therapy.

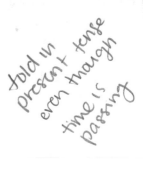

told in present tense even though time is passing

Patient turns twenty-five and her wonderful, previously omnipresent health insurance coughs a warning death-rattle. Patient feels—she doesn't know what she feels. She wonders, as she did five years earlier, if she needs her medication. She asks her therapist, whom she likes very much, for a referral back to us, *just to see.* This is insincere; Patient knows what she wants but she also knows to stop a medication she's been taking for seven years *cold turkey* is *straight-up stupid.* Patient is referred back into our care.

Patient does not like us in in our new form. Our office is obscenely large and the furniture is made of studded leather that, at this point, Patient is certain comes standard-issue with every private practice. Even greater than Patient's dislike of us is Patient's dislike of her own medical history. She hates how it sounds coming out of her mouth: *Yes, but* —. Her defenses are weak against our volley of questions: *Hospitalized for a psychiatric disturbance? History of drug abuse? Self-harm/suicidal ideation? Multiple sexual partners? Disordered eating? Are you sleeping? How are your moods? Your energy levels?* Patient couches her answers in graduate school: Everyone is tired, eats poorly, etc. We sit with one pantyhosed leg crossed over the other and ask Patient if she is sure she wants to *decrease* her bipolar medication, even though we both know it is the reason Patient came in. It is a rhetorical question, a lead-in to our claim: *It seems* to us that Patient *isn't even stable now.* Patient smiles. She is learning the value of her dimpled cheeks. Patient is polite. Patient speaks calmly, says, she's *curious* and she's *in therapy* and leans upon her therapist's praises for us. Patient is patient. We write her a new prescription, eking down the dosage.

During this withdrawal, no one needs to point out the Patient's irritability. *Irritable* is too mild a word. Patient waits in line at the grocery store at the coffee shop at the—those are actually the only two places she goes—and finds herself seething, chestnut-sized lumps in her cheeks where her jawbones meet. Patient tells her roommate about it because she's confused, there's *no reason for it*. But it is summer and it is beautiful outdoors and the undirected anger passes.

Patient tells us, when asked how the new dosage is working, that things are *good*. A thought intercedes: Individuals with bipolar mania sometimes stop taking their medication. So Patient hedges, is more truthful, mentions the disturbances at the initial decrease, calls it *irritation* rather than *hatred*. We are surprised by what she reports. We expected something more dramatic. Patient smiles. We write Patient another prescription.

Patient calls her friend in the middle of the night. He answers with a normal *Hello?* though this isn't a normal phone call. Patient is kneeling on the floor of her living room. She sobs, keeps sobbing. Her friend asks what is wrong; he is concerned, maybe even frightened, because she moves through the daylight with bravado and swagger, all extroversion and arrogance; a new, hard rage keeps her upright like a concrete support beam. Patient says, *I can't*, keeps repeating the phrase. She is hiccuping now. *Can't what?* her friend asks. Patient is bent in half—her face is pressed into her knees so hard that afterward there will be marks on her cheeks and forehead, like pillow lines. Her sobs continue, the repetition continues. Eventually, Patient manages two more words, though no more information: *I just fucking can't*. Her friend cannot fix what she is feeling, and she knows it, maybe even knew it before she called. Her brain is recalibrating.

In the middle of baking a loaf of lemon poppy seed bread—the speckled batter still in the bowl, not yet in the tin— Patient slumps to the floor. More despair.

Patient sleepwalks through the mornings and afternoons, until nighttime when she feels energized, an inverse morning glory or sunflower.

Patient tells her therapist what is happening, and she tells her therapist she is going to lie to us about it. Patient *doesn't trust* us. Patient looks at her therapist, earnest, seeking permission to deceive. Patient is afraid. The *withdrawal is hell* but if she were to stop now then—what? With every passing day, despite her weeping, Patient suspects more and more she is not sick in the way we'd diagnosed her.

During her third visit to us, Patient smiles and reiterates *everything is fine*. We say it's as if Patient and *this woman* (we gesture to Patient's file, a manila folder containing her medical history) are *two completely different people*. Patient nods, smiles some more. *It's as if*, Patient echoes. She is a small bird now, and she sees an open window. She takes the new script in her mouth, flies through it.

For Halloween, Patient dresses like Alex from Stanley Kubrick's *A Clockwork Orange*, minus the codpiece. At a party, she worries she is drinking spiked punch and cannot shake the idea. It grows, sucks up into her lungs like vines, takes away her breath.

Patient splits her pills in half, as we instructed. She uses her fingers, breaks the chalky white along the scored line. It is a familiar motion.

A levee springs a slow leak. Maybe twice a week, Patient throws up her dinner. Maybe less. Maybe more.

Mood stabilizer is (successfully?) eliminated. Patient has split the last pill, taken the final half. She goes to bed for the first time in seven years without any amount of this medication in her system. It is the first time in ten years she has gone to bed without any amount of any medication. Patient asks her therapist if she was *misdiagnosed.* Her therapist avoids the word. Her therapist says instead she *doesn't think* Patient has bipolar disorder.

AFTER

Patient remains wary.

What might Patient do now that she knows she is living without mental illness? *Misdiagnosed.* The word feels funny inside her mouth.

Patient's therapist gives her a clean bill of health.

As Patient prepares to move across the country (again), her anxiety redoubles. It arrives in the form of obsessive thoughts related to her physical health and safety. Online message boards describe the withdrawal process from this medicine as *the worst thing, ever*. She hears a story about a woman who was *fucked up for years* after stopping antidepressants.

Self-pity is not a likable or admirable trait. Patient wants to say she does not *feel sorry* for herself and mean it. Patient spent so much time ashamed of a sickness that wasn't real that now she swings in the opposite direction, showing everyone her insides tacked out like an animal on the dissection table. See here? This is the liver. The small intestine. The heart.

The new phase of thinking is forced dichotomies: *either* Patient had bipolar disorder *or* Patient acted like such a selfish asshole that everyone (including us) believed she must have a mental illness.

Patient's anxieties follow her to an ashram. Her car becomes a flammable trap made of metal, the other visitors are carriers of pathogens. She fears sudden, inexplicable death—freak accidents. Patient does not throw up, but wants to. She sneaks off the property late at night to smoke the cigarettes she swore off.

Lyme disease. Brain cancer. Blown Tire. HIV. Drunkenness. West Nile. Blown Tire. Lung cancer. MS. They are tiresome in their redundancies.

In her new city, Patient returns to us. For once, our office has no leather chairs. The windows are opaque with condensation and prickly caterpillars carpet the sidewalks. We ask about Patient's medical history, and Patient says she was *misdiagnosed bipolar*, took the meds for seven years, stopped taking them *eight months* prior. We suck our teeth, look perturbed. The Patient cannot tell which of her anxiety is situational and which is pathological. She asks for medication—not *the good stuff*, not the *benzos*—something she could take every day. We write a prescription for an SSRI.

The new pills make Patient nauseated. She is too sick and too tired to be anxious. She cannot orgasm. Her sleep schedule reverses: She naps during the day, falls asleep immediately at night, wakes every few hours until morning.

During her follow-up appointment, Patient says, *I don't think this is supposed to happen.* Patient describes her side effects. We ask why she didn't stop taking the pills sooner. Patient shrugs, says she thought it would *get better.* When we ask if Patient wants to try a different medication, Patient refuses, though not unkindly. She offers us a gummy cherry from a bag in her lap. We demur, saying we *cannot take food* from patients. Patient smiles because she is no longer our patient, and says so. We take the candy. SSRI is ~~ineffective~~ eliminated.

Patient has moved from dichotomy to plurality— each actor (Patient, all our manifestations, Patient's family and friends) affected by their own ideas from books, from television, from science, from music, from who-knows-where, of what mental illness is and does and how *nice girls* from *good families* are supposed to behave. Factored thusly, it's incalculable, the equation.

At a conference in Portugal, Patient is just now comfortable enough to breathe the word *misdiagnosis* in the open Atlantic air. She reads an essay aloud that features her trip to the psych ward. A woman she knows, but not well, comes up to her afterward, while they are freezing on a cobblestoned plaza overlooking a beautiful skyline, and says that *the same thing* happened to her brother. He was so much better off the meds. Patient doesn't smile yet, but she nods and nods and nods.

go ask alice

At least once you should live with someone
more medicated than yourself...
– Bob Hicok, "Bottom of the Ocean"

Alice kept a shoebox full of pills in her closet, and there were still more orange bottles lined up on our bathroom sink. Every morning and night, her phone pinged with medication reminders, offering convenient checkboxes to keep track of it all. Sometimes she forgot to mark off the doses (or did she? she was never sure), and those were the watching days.

We met at the start of graduate school, orientation as a predictable gray sludge of complicated policies that would be half-heartedly enforced and painful icebreakers—Two Truths! And One Lie!—orchestrated by earnest-faced model students. Alice and I were foils that day: I talked too much; she said almost nothing. After eight hours together at a small, round table, I'd learned only that she preferred Earl Grey tea and planned to attend the optional, informational session the next day.

So it wasn't a surprise the following afternoon when, as I entered the large university auditorium, I saw Alice curled up in a chair close to the stage. It was impossible to feign not noticing her, and I sat down.

"Hey."

"Hi."

Either I'd arrived close to the assembly's beginning or I've mercifully forgotten what awkward, stilted conversation we shared in waiting. But what happened next is important. The speaker was terrible, and so instead of listening or even pretending to listen, I studied Alice. I took in her rainbowed leopard-print backpack; her small feet, covered in thin cotton socks; the slip-on shoes she'd wedged underneath her chair; the thin script tattoos on her wrists. Pale, pale scars tracked up the inside of her left arm that matched those on my right.

Though she doesn't remember this, Alice later told me it was our mutual love of strong, dark tea that suggested to her we would be friends. For me, it was the scars.

When the speaker announced we'd be moving into capital-B Break-Out Sessions according to research interests and resource concerns, Alice and I looked at one another and agreed to slip out while everyone else was regrouping. We walked across the red-bricked campus slowly, feeling sticky in the August afternoon.

A smiling man, blond and wholesome-looking, stood in front of a blue-and-white tent and asked if we wanted a snow cone.

"I don't have cash," I mock-wailed.

"They're free," he answered.

I raised my eyebrows at Alice, and she nodded in agreement.

As another man inside the tent pumped blue raspberry sugar over shaved ice, the smiling one began the pitch for his Christian campus organization.

"Oh," I said, eyeing my almost-ready snow cone.

"Have you heard of us?" he asked.

"No, no," I said, looking back at Alice, who was shaking her head.

"Well—" he began.

We couldn't bring ourselves to walk away until he had finished his bit, we but politely declined his offer for more information.

Afterward, when our mouths were dyed blue and green (Alice had chosen lime), we agreed the sweets had been an excellent lure and worth listening to the pitch. "Snow cones for Jesus!" would have been much less effective. We giggled like the new graduate students we were, tired of playing grown-up, relieved to find someone with whom we could drop the pretense.

Even though individuals with mental illness are more likely to harm themselves than anyone else, the press and popular culture often suggest otherwise. Rhetoric and disabilities scholar Margaret Price, when examining media coverage of the Virginia Tech and Northern Illinois University shooters, found that "madness is generally assumed to be the *cause* of [their] actions." One of the troubles with this, she concludes, is that it creates a false dichotomy, suggesting "madness and sanity are two extremely separate spaces—one dangerous and one safe." We want so badly to be okay that all nuances disappear. More distressingly, Price continues, the public often extrapolates from this type of reporting "that all persons with mental disabilities are potential threats." It's not necessary to read academic scholarship to notice this. There are so many examples in recent news reports following mass shootings by white gunmen (and each time I revisit this draft there's a new one to look at that supports this argument) and in nearly all procedural crime dramas produced in the United States. Despite my lived experience and book-knowledge, I still can't completely override the hours of *Law & Order* and *Criminal Minds* I've pumped into my brain.

It wasn't surprising when a student in my composition course turned in a hastily written essay that made distressing and inaccurate claims about school shootings and insanity. It is so easy to be afraid, and so hard to admit to it. Two weeks after the rash of school shootings in October of 2015 (Umpqua Community College in Oregon, Northern Arizona University, Texas Southern University, Tennessee State University), an unfamiliar young white man walked into my university classroom. His dark hair, heavy with grease, covered his face like wet palm fronds. A black t-shirt hung off his bony clavicles. Head tilted down, eyes focused on the floor, he ignored my too-high-pitched, "May I help you?" I panicked as he moved about the classroom, his mouth opening and closing like a fish. My thoughts skipped and sputtered. *Is he looking for someone in particular? Do any of my students recognize him? Why have I never programmed campus security's number into my phone?* After a minute, he turned around and left without acknowledging anyone. My stomach loosened itself and dropped.

My students snickered. "What the fuck was that?" they whispered.

Irritated with myself, I wanted to shush them like errant children.

It's possible the man was just hungover. I want to say I've never looked so frighteningly out of place as he did that day, but this is untrue. I've just tucked the memories away—the hours I've sat in crowded rooms drumming my fingers on tables, bouncing my legs up and down, muttering, fiending; vomiting while walking across neon-green suburban lawns; passing out in stockrooms in the middle of afternoon work shifts; walking up to people in their cars to say their gas cap was open only to watch them recoil from my body, my badly dyed hair, and the metal piercing my face, like I was dangerous.

The first night of our off-campus friendship began when I invited myself to Alice's apartment with a dish of eggplant Parmesan. I'd wanted to have her at my place but lived with a man who was often gone and nervous about people—whom he termed *strangers*—in the house without him present. And so I went to Alice's. We sat on the couch, and a chunky black cat twined around my legs before hurling herself into my lap as Alice and I watched *Ghost Hunters.*

"Why is he speaking English? Aren't the ghosts German?" I asked.

"Medieval German, too."

"Must be why they're not appearing."

"The language barrier. Obviously."

We ended the night on her balcony exchanging stories. Alice told me about her first kiss, which took place—here's Bob Hicok again—

> *where windows are mesh and what's sharp*
> *is banished and what can be thrown*
> *is attached so unless you can lift*
> *the whole building everyone is safe.*

I knew the setting well. We laughed hard together, our breath white and cloudy with cigarette smoke and the Midwest weather just starting to turn.

As the year closed, my relationship with the man I lived with unraveled quickly. In a fit of serendipity, Alice's then-roommate broke the lease and returned home, leaving behind an extra bedroom that needed filling. I emailed Alice during the holidays: *If I leave him, can I move in with you?* She said, *Yes*, and one month later I showed up at her door with only ten minutes' notice, not speaking, eyes full of tears. She lent me a pair of pajama pants with blue-eyed cartoon leopards, drove me to CVS to buy a toothbrush, and her home became our home.

My bipolar I diagnosis began in a locked state psychiatric hospital. Once considered unsound of mind, all protestations to the contrary are further evidence of delusion or instability. The deadbolt turns another terrifying click.

As popular culture dictates that mad men have the guns and the inherent capacity for violence, it also dictates that mad women should be locked away. Consider the classic examples of Charlotte Perkins Gilman's "The Yellow Wallpaper" or Susanna Kaysen's *Girl, Interrupted*. In both instances, though the protagonists are misdiagnosed, the unease surrounding deviant women proves so extreme that their consequences are the same regardless. These fears that surround mental illness, Price argues, result in a culture where people "are stripped of their rights and further stigmatized, and the very real violence . . . they face is ignored." Literally locking someone away makes them more akin to a zoo animal than a person; decisions are made *for their own good*. This is how the dehumanization starts. Diagnoses become labels that determine futures. Michel Foucault writes, "Our society does not wish to recognize itself in the ill individual whom it rejects or locks up; as it diagnoses the illness, it excludes the patient." To see ourselves in others is terrifying because it suggests we must be kind, always. Instead, we invent stories, familiar and comfortable, to distance ourselves from the mentally ill: the trope of the unbalanced artist, the narrative of overcoming, the sick as a recipient of charity who provides an uplifting moral lesson. We can imagine whatever we want when we are removed from the subject, which then becomes the object of our thoughts.

This isn't to say I'm any more evolved. After staying in a psych ward, I did everything I could to ensure I'd never return. I took the pills, learned to fry French toast and clean the shower grout, attended therapy, re-enrolled in school, and tucked and picked and shaped myself to resemble what I believed passed for a Real Girl. A sane woman. I held my pose like a sculpture, terrified to move, afraid my body would give me away.

Soon after I moved in with her, I learned how sad Alice could get and how the winters made it worse. On cold mornings I crawled into her twin bed, pushed aside a pile of animals, rubbed her back, made jokes about playing cat-Tetris, and cajoled her into getting up for work. Expressing concern made her weeping markedly worse; the best thing to do, she said, was to pretend like it wasn't happening. So I made stupid puns and complained, usually about the cold weather or the other grad students, until she laughed.

It was some frozen night when I first saw her spoon cold Campbell's vegetable soup straight from the can to her mouth. My jaw hung open like the metal pull-tab lid.

"What the shit are you eating?" I asked.

"Soup," she said, dragging out the u-sound, long and plaintive.

"That," I said, "is not actually soup."

Directly on the table were also two plain tortillas and a small plate with a dollop of sour cream.

Alice had been diagnosed with depression at a young age, but while we lived together this was amended to bipolar II, which offered her hope because different medications are often used to treat the diagnosis. Alice was prescribed one drug. Then another, in tandem. Then off one, on another. Then on again. I'd come home from class and she'd be on the couch playing video games with an ice pack wrapped onto her forehead with a scarf. She named her Pokemon after psychotropic medications, enjoying the battle script: *Depakote used "stun!" It's super- effective!*

Trying to find the correct psychiatric medication can be a time-consuming and difficult process because the pills take a few weeks to build up in the body and start working their neurotransmitter magic. Every headache, every yawn, is a possible side effect; every mood change is subject to a question of causality. The medication made Alice tired. She had always been able to nap whenever and wherever, but she began to sleep an incredible amount, what seemed like ten or twelve hours for every twenty-four. She was a less claustrophobic and better-tempered version of the roommate in Hicok's poem who is

> *. . . sealed in amber, a caul*
> *of drugs meant to withstand ants and fire*

Outside the apartment, we carried on. Alice sometimes disappeared from class or from our afternoon writing sessions for ten-minute intervals, returning with red eyes and a stuffy nose. We ate brunch on Sundays at a restaurant with a weekly rotating menu and butcher-paper tablecloths on which we doodled our various crises in primary-colored crayon cartoons. During the week, I assigned my students texts about ethnicity, gender, sexuality, ability, class, age. Though I stood at the front of the classroom clearly a woman, clearly not white, I never announced that in addition to those obvious facets of my identity, I took a diamond-shaped pill every night before bed to ensure that I would return to them, rather than a locked ward, each week. I am unsure how we are to move past our conceptions of mental illness, both gendered and not, because it still carries such stigma. To offer ourselves up in cupped hands, both supplicant and giver.

Winter turned into spring turned into summer, and after holding the posture of Real Girl for such a long time, I grew tired. What if everyone was wrong? The doctors, my family, my friends, me? I'd been diagnosed so young. What if the easiest explanation for a girl like me, wild wild wild, was illness? One day, instead of going home to Alice and the cats, I drove an hour south to see a doctor. This began the six-month process of weaning off the bipolar medication I'd taken every day for seven years.

The last few months were the hardest. The body reacts badly to withdrawal. After each dosage decrease, I'd spend two weeks like a simmering pot of water, the slight tremor in my hands an expression of directionless rage. I was debilitated by anxiety. I felt like I was losing control of my body again: I slept little and threw up my meals. I wept. Alice took care of me: She drove me home when I panicked in public, she made me coffee after bouts of insomnia, she told jokes to make me laugh, and in December it was finally over. Unlike the roommate in Hicok's poem who

> *. . . because he'd not taken*
> *the microwave apart and strapped its heart*
> *to his head or talked to the 60-watt bulb*
> *on the porch he thought he was better*
> *and flushed his pills . . .*

and ended up back in a psychiatric facility, my body righted after my brain adjusted to its new balance. I was officially of sound mind, transported back to the kingdom of the well. Though the journey was slow, once I'd arrived the view was jarring. I looked back over the previous ten years askance, squinting over the peaks and valleys I'd gone through.

Alice and I sat on her old blue futon, her legs crossed beneath her, mine up on the coffee table. That same needy black cat twined around us, wanting, while another sat on top of a five-story bookshelf, yowling down. For the first time in my adult life, I was free of psychiatric medication. I went to bed with a phantom itch on the back of my neck, feeling like I was forgetting something.

It was winter again. The backs of my hands splintered with small white lines and the skin around my fingers peeled back from the cold, dry air. Alice picked her lips and played a mindless counting game on her computer while I babbled, interrupting both her and myself, trying to make sense.

"Do you think I could make myself"—I made air quotes with my fingers—"'crazy' again? Or is this it, I'm just done and safe forever?" Always veering between two extremes.

"I mean," Alice started, "I'm sure you could do things that would wreck your life like—"

"Getting strung out again?" I offered.

"Or deprive yourself of sleep, or stop eating."

"For example," I said.

For seven years I'd lived afraid of my own mind, both what it was capable of and what others would think and do if they found out about it, only to learn it had been a mistake. An error. Disability scholar Lennard J. Davis furthers Foucault's claims about society's distancing itself from the ill to say, "in a society where the concept of the norm is operative, then people with disabilities will be thought of as deviants." I think the statement is still true with the second half reversed—*in a society where the concept of the norm is operative, those who deviate from its expectations may be (mis)diagnosed as ill.*

It seems that misdiagnosis is more common than I imagined or than my doctors were willing to express. A study published in the *Journal of Clinical Psychiatry* in 2008— one year after my bipolar I diagnosis—found that out of a sampling of 700 psychiatric outpatients, about twenty percent had been diagnosed at some time with bipolar disorder. Of that twenty percent, fewer than half met the criteria for the illness when re-evaluated. The study's authors called this identification "an overdiagnosis." Doctor were overcorrecting for an earlier trend of delayed and *under*diagnosing bipolar. Add a young woman with a habit of stimulants and specious ideas about mental health to the mix, and perhaps it's easy to see where I fell in with my diagnosis.

My initial temptation after learning that was to lean back satisfied, sigh, and say, *Ah, that's it then.* We read true stories of trauma and illness like step-by-step guides to overcoming, but if I've learned anything from my misdiagnosis, it's that our understanding of reality (because that's all that we have, really, our understanding of it, rather than the thing itself) is constantly in flux and any stasis is either illusive or temporary. I still don't know what to do about this. We're constantly evolving—fins into hands, gills into lungs.

Some years after we lived together, Alice and I met up and tried to attend a Bob Hicok reading in Los Angeles. Our plans failed miserably. I ran late, and Hicok didn't show—a family emergency. Alice slunk out as surreptitiously as possible (she still has that rainbow leopard-print backpack) once his cancellation was announced.

She later joked, "I'd postponed a nap for this."

I told her a secondhand anecdote, passed down to me from another writer, of Hicok refusing to give a reading in a crowded, underground bar. Hicok arrived, saw the tightly packed mass of people, and promptly exited. What courage it takes to say, *This is too much.* What courage it takes to leave.

Later that night, after the failed reading, Alice and I sprawled across twin beds in our shared hotel room talking about the role of an artist. What were our responsibilities, how might we deal with representation in an ethical manner, where did we find community in our new lives—endless questions with no definitive answers for either of us. Despite all that had changed in the time between for both of us, I felt like I'd come home. I bit at the skin around my fingernails in lieu of smoking cigarettes. Alice worked on her novel. To go back to Hicok one last time:

. . . I learned you can sit
with someone who's on the bottom
of the ocean and not get wet

but my clothes are stiff like they've been dipped in seawater,
and there are strands of kelp still knotted in my hair.

unsent

We don't look alike, but set against the backdrop of that small, Midwestern city, we could have been sisters. I nicknamed the town *la misère blanche* (population 68,000) for the dirty snow piled high as the streetlights in strip mall parking lots and packed into ice on the unplowed roads. How did we end up in such a place? It was more livable the rest of the year, but even in summer, potholed streets dug their hungry teeth into our car and bicycle tires. The asphalt's cracks worsened each spring as the ice thawed, seeping into crevices and refreezing.

When I first arrived in the city, I lived with a local who told me stories about its history. He said it had been one of the most segregated places in the nation. In high school, he said he could draw a line down the middle of the lunchroom and it would be split into Black and White halves. I don't know whether this was hyperbole or not. I think he meant to charm me or, at least, to explain our home, but instead my distrust of the sprawling soybean plants and aggressively gorgeous sunsets deepened. A co-worker approached me a few days into a gig waiting tables at a chain restaurant. I'd noticed her before. She was brown-eyed and thin, and her hair was all tight ringlets.

"Are you mixed?" she asked.

"Mixed?" I echoed.

It was like a David Ives play.

"Yeah, mixed," she repeated.

"Yeah, mixed," I said.

She clapped her hands. "I'm not the only mixed girl anymore!"

I must've smiled.

A year later, when I met you in that downtown bar with fried pickles and a surprisingly good beer selection, I flashed back to that echoing exchange. Might you and I become friends based on nothing but vaguely similar features—dark eyes and hair, skin that took well to sunlight, rounded noses and high cheeks—*exotic* women, affinity based in isolation?

To write down all the times I failed to defend myself while living in the Midwest would take longer than I have energy for. The town wore me down until the sounds of train horns no longer woke me at night.

These aren't excuses. These are excuses.

Our first semester teaching, one of my students, a redhead who had, before this moment, impressed me with his wit, said about you, "She reminds me of an Eskimo."

"What?" I asked.

"You know." He made a gesture to indicate a large hood bundled around his face so only his eyes and nose were visible.

My face moved all by itself, but no sounds came out.

He held his hands up, palms out. "Oh wow, okay," he said.

It didn't start well, did it? I am still much less than I would like to be.

•

I wrote my first letters when I was ten, maybe eleven. Do you remember those gel pens from the '90s—offensively bright and hard to read in pink and lime green? My left hand smudged the ink as it moved across the page. I wonder how the results were legible. Email had begun to sneak into its position as the best way to communicate across oceans, but I was sentimental even then. If glass bottles could have reliably traversed the Atlantic, I would have used hundreds. I find the physical shaping of letters more romantic than the tap-tap-tap of a keyboard. It takes more effort, which says something disconcerting about my ideas of love. I still kiss important envelopes before slipping them into the mailbox.

Back then, I'd write at my desk and eat kilos of clementines in a single sitting. I practiced removing the peel in one piece, biting near the stem and making small circles around the fruit's circumference with my thumb and pointer finger. I'd bite my fingers, too, and peel my nails down, down, down, by the millimeter, as low as I could stand, then lower, once they'd healed enough to touch.

These early-life letters were sent to a friend who'd remained at home while my family moved overseas. In retrospect, we didn't like each other much (at least, we didn't act like we did), but we had the same birthday and were at the age where such synchronicity suggested that we should be friends.

I haven't learned much, it seems.

When we next saw each other, it was summertime and we were just-shy-of-teenagers and fully immersed in hating ourselves: growth spurts, hormones, scrunchies. We stopped writing soon after. I remember her face, her shirt textured like a towel, the broken-heart best friend necklace, the stories that circled years later of how she'd developed an eating disorder and been taken away. I'd wanted to be just like her. I hope she's well. I hope you're well, too.

It wasn't just our facial features that were the same. We shared other traits I wouldn't admit to having. For example: the way we loved men. First, we picked ones who loved us solidly, and then, when we'd become dissatisfied, we'd seek out others for whom we'd shatter ourselves trying to get their attention. We waved our arms, stamped our feet like little girls crying out, *See this; see me.* It's not an attractive look.

To watch you break yourself open upon the altar of another human was difficult. I know it was harder for you to do it, and I'm sorry I still struggle with stepping outside myself. Seeing your wanting was like staring in a mirror: I remembered hallucinating ringtones and my stomach growling from skipped dinners. To distance myself, I kept a running list of our differences—the particulars aren't important. Its purpose was only to convince myself that I was better than you. I wanted no reminders of the woman I used to be, the woman I worried I could become again if presented with the right set of circumstances. It's hard to look back.

In rehab, my drug counselor told me to write a letter to a person whom I deeply resented. I immediately began to resent my counselor. She was a pale woman who wore bright pink lipstick and cut her dyed-black hair into a severe pageboy. The point of the assignment, she claimed, was the writing, not the sending.

•

The idea behind this practice is an old one: parsing complex emotions by their articulation. Good old catharsis. In the case of written expression, a person can literally see their thoughts, instead of merely thinking them, which may enable a more balanced perspective—as if looking at a pair of glasses rather than seeing through their lenses.

Of course, I didn't write the letter. The next time I saw my counselor, I glared at her over her desk and acted like I'd learned something. The leather chair squeaked beneath my fidgeting.

"I get it," I said. "We're the same—that's why I'm so angry. I don't like myself either."

She nodded, seeming pleased. My performance must have worked because she didn't press me to write it, regardless of what I thought I'd find.

Eleven years later, this is what I know: Writing exposes the weaknesses in our thought patterns (what we take for granted) and also surprises (what we didn't know we were hiding from ourselves). I was not ready to look at myself, the way I'd curled up around my bitterness. That letter remains unwritten.

Did they try to make you do this too? I bet they did.

Do you remember the night you came over and rolled around on the living room carpet? It was an uncertain shade of taupe and matted with cat fur and litter, but you didn't grimace. Your commitment to self-destruction was both familiar and admirable. You talked nonstop without saying anything, typed paragraph-long replies to concerned commenters on your vague social media posts, chewed painkillers—roll, roll,

roll. Was this before or after the accident, before or after you disappeared into a psychiatric facility? I can't remember. Was it sometime between the two events? Or am I mixing up your story with mine?

I wanted to throw you out of my apartment and into the summer sky. Into the stars and the soybean fields. Instead, I retreated to my bedroom and shut the door.

Have I ever told you about the time I swallowed too much Prozac with a few mouthfuls of Crown whiskey and told the boy who'd hurt me I'd taken more of both? How I walked miles through suburban neighborhoods, through woods? Of course I haven't told you. I ran through oaks and pines, hoping I'd trip over a root and break a bone. I wanted to throw myself down a hill that ended in rocks and water, but my body wouldn't let go. Every time I fell, my hands and knees caught just right. The survival instinct runs too deeply in me. My palms were barely scraped.

Eventually, I caught a ride from a stranger sprawled in a driveway. He drove me to that boy's best friend's house. I'd sleep with the best friend when I arrived, maybe that day or another, but wouldn't tell the boy himself. You'd think that would be the point, wouldn't you? To fuck his best friend and then tell him, to wound him? But I kept the secret. I worked the grit that settled in my chest over and over with bile until it shone like a pearl, a second heart that hurt but I guarded nonetheless.

After a few years of this, all grown up, I took a deep breath and cracked open my ribs to show off my secret. My bravery was less than I'd anticipated. The boy, by then all grown up too, told me that he'd known for a long time. Now you know, too.

•

I now send and receive more letters than I can count. The last one that came in the mail was tied with red satin ribbon and a fake miniature rose. A surprising number of people are as sentimental as I am, and we have found each other. I have received through personal correspondence, among other gifts, a small piece of a European city, shake (this was an accident), whole-bean coffee and a hand-grinder, a teddy bear wearing a shirt expressing love for the United States Air Force, a zine whose cover features a picture of my friend in the bath, blueberry jam, a green Che Guevara cap (with a note saying I was to wear it only indoors), and a pretend monocle. I don't keep everything, but I wish I could. I am amazed by these small tokens, how they move from one place to another, ending with me.

I think the word I am looking for is gratitude. I am grateful, though it has taken me years to unearth the feeling from beneath the garbage. I'm talking about the real stuff here, not the bullshit we say when we're scared and locked up so the counselors and doctors will leave us alone. I'm talking about the gratitude that comes after the suffering, after its attendant bitterness and the remorse. The gratitude that lets us look and see.

indie night
at the goth club

See the Notes section for an accompanying playlist.

At The Castle in Ybor City, Thursday nights slipped into Friday mornings like easy exhales. It's not where I imagined I'd be spending my late twenties, but I couldn't stay away. Nearly thirty years after its construction in 1992, The Castle is still notorious for its counterculture scene: Fridays are billed as Midnight Mass ("gothic and industrial"), Saturdays are called Carpe Noctem ("dark electronic"), and posters in the bathrooms advertise cosplay and sexdoll events. The building's exterior looks like a cartoon fortress, turret and all. At least one person has allegedly asked for their ashes to be scattered on its premises. On Thursdays they played indie pop.

Entering The Castle was akin to a goth middle schooler's choose-your-own-adventure fantasy: You walk through a wooden door that is rounded at the top and covered in ironwork reminiscent of a generic medieval time period. Once inside, you are eye level with posters of naked men while an actual one checks your ID, stamps your hand, and affixes a wristband that indicates whether or not you can legally drink alcohol. Overhead, red lights glint off a plastic chandelier. It's decision time. Ahead of you are wide, carpeted stairs leading up to the second floor; to the left is the dungeon where a pentagram of bones hangs above the DJ stand; to the right is a stone-topped bar. Each space has its own set of music playing, and beneath the chandelier the sounds blur together so only the bass' thrum is distinguishable. Which way do you go?

There was an element of ritual to my Thursdays, and after so much repetition the nights have blurred together like a movie: idealized and forever in the present tense. As 10 p.m. rolls around, we—Mark, Felicity, Arizona, and I— slowly begin to congregate at Arizona's apartment. She is the linchpin of our group, and her living room is well lit, with high ceilings and framed Modest Mouse posters and a Pantone palette calendar in shades of blue. We finish getting dressed: eyeliner, kitten stockings, dog collars. My friends pull down hard cider and vegetarian Jell-O shots that aren't set. I gulp Red Bulls and chain-smoke. The mood is expansive. I drive.

Mark shouts from the back seat during the thirty-minute trip downtown. Once we arrive at The Castle, the night's film splits into one of two scenarios. The first: Mark sings along with the hair band hits, *Love shack, bay-beeeeee.* He drags his hands from his face to his waistband, he pushes his hands through his floppy bangs, he clenches his hands into fists and pulls them toward his body, *Why don't we give ourselves one more chance?* The more he drinks, the more his movements loosen. While Arizona, Felicity, and I remain clustered on the dance floor, refusing eye contact with all men, Mark flops onto the empty stage beneath a large flatscreen playing music videos. He then gets up and makes laps around the top story of the club—passing the St. Andrew's cross and the Gothic windows, weaving around the go-go dancers on raised plexiglass platforms who move as if through water, lit from beneath in a blinking redbluredbblueredblue—propelled by that inexplicable drunken inertia. We ask if he is okay, and Mark insists he is fine, he is fine, he is fine, before sitting down in a corner and falling asleep. This is our cue to leave, gathering up Mark and placing him in my car's passenger seat.

The second scenario: Mark doesn't pace around the club, but instead remains in our circle on the dance floor, and we stay until the lights come up. Though Thursdays are advertised as Indie Night, the playlist is based on contemporary requests with some nods to the late '70s and '80s: think Iggy Azalea to Iggy Pop. Arizona twirls to her favorite songs, *So, yeah, we're werewolves*, stepping gracefully in white platform shoes. When the floor suddenly clears in a herd movement toward the bar, she shimmies across the open space, elbows swinging, taking up as much room as she can, laughing, *Why you looking at me now?* She swings her long hair.

Felicity is immaculate, the easiest of us to love. She radiates patience. At the bar, she smiles politely to men who insist that they are interesting; on the dance floor, she raises her eyebrows in perfect, non-judgmental surprise at the music's sudden genre shifts. She is also the only one of us who can actually execute a dance move. Her favorite songs are pop hits, *Nobody pray for me*, the ones playing on the radio that I've never heard before. "I don't know this," I shout again and again. She tells me the artists and song titles, gracious. She dips, *It can only mean one thing*, bends, smiles contentedly at her own movements like a cat curled in a patch of warm laundry. I am lucky to have friends who will keep dancing when the lights go up halfway through the night's last song, even though we can see one another.

One of the smartest men I know is a cartoonist and a former member of a Nü Metal band. He once told me that the music we listen to in our adolescence remains a master key that forever unlocks the emotional frequencies of that decade. I replied, "Uh-oh," and avoided eye contact.

As a teenager, I liked music with a fast tempo—the kind best listened to loud. Nuance of sound has never been my forte. My first concert was Slayer, one of the most well-known thrash metal bands. They've been around since the early '80s and in many ways exemplify the genre's stereotypes. It's possible to buy stickers and placards mimicking the hand-washing dictums in public restrooms that read, *Employees Must Carve Slayer Into Forearms Before Returning to Work.* A pentagram replaces the usual image of lathered hands. Imagine me at sixteen, dressed for the show: dark pants with ragged cuffs, dog collar, rings upon cheap rings, leather cords around my neck with brass alchemy symbols. At the show, meaty men in their forties wearing black cutoff t-shirts politely kept me from falling beneath the press of the crowd when "Raining Blood" began. When I ran into the mosh pit, my friend's swinging fist glanced off my cheekbone, and the next day at school, I ran at him, jumped, and held on. A few years later, Jeff Hammond, the guitarist, contracted a case of flesh-eating bacteria. Slayer's shows have always been like this; a 1998 review in *The New York Times* describes the concert experience as "no more or less interesting than watching an enormous furnace for 90 minutes." The "pleasure" of it, the review reads, is "purely physical." That last sentence is obvious though. Humans have always known that catharsis comes when bodies move through space.

A few years later, I saw Tool play in a massive sports arena in Richmond. Like Slayer, the band has been criticized for their disturbing lyrics, though this hasn't stopped them from also winning Grammys. Tool's music is trippy. The titular song from their album *Lateralus* takes its time signatures and lyrics from the Fibonacci sequence. A ten-minute music video for their song "Parabol/Parabola" features stop-motion animation and imagery drawn from Kundalini yoga. I watched it with friends after eating two gel tabs and wandering through the woods, and someone said, maybe out loud or maybe not, *It's like they're showing what's in my head.*

At the time of the Tool concert, I was living in a near-stranger's house in a small town on the water. A cop pulled us over on our way to the show. The van we rode in was oversized and white, more suitable for construction equipment than passengers. Most days, blue vodka bottles rolled around beneath the seats every time the brakes engaged. The cop asked, nicely, to search the vehicle and didn't look too hard. Since he didn't find anything, I barely remember the concert. We were to the left of the stage, up in the seats. There were blue lights, smoke, drums, Maynard. That night, I almost went home with another stranger.

That night, I fired a gun into the night off the highway for fun. The first single off Tool's *Undertow* album is titled "Sober." Maynard mumbles in the outro, *I want what I want, I want what I want.* I worry that if The Cartoonist is right this means I will always feel needlessly pitted against the world.

•

I'd first heard of The Castle a decade before becoming a Thursday-night regular. The place had mythos. An ex's friend, who worked as a dominatrix, spent weekends there with her clients. Later, my college friends would tell me convoluted stories of their late nights there. I'd listen and sigh and then, as soon as classes ended, head in the opposite direction of Ybor, driving home over a ten-mile bridge. The Castle pulled at my imagination, but I stayed away. As embarrassing and dramatic as it sounds now: I was afraid.

The aesthetics of my adolescence had swung violently between having too many feelings and wanting to have absolutely none, and the inevitable fallout resulted in an over-commitment to responsibility. I quit doing the fun drugs and started taking the right ones. I moved down the Eastern Seaboard. I went back to school full-time the semester before my twenty-first birthday. I arranged my new life in such a way that no conditions could lead to relapse—of either substance or mood. No more powder, no more late nights, no more psych wards. This was, I thought, the task of becoming a real girl, of growing up and getting well: working and working and working until my restless energy was spent, not having too much fun lest it tip into another dangerous upward spiral.

My adolescent CD collection was full of Tipper Gore's Parental Advisory stickers. I also kicked holes in my bedroom walls. In some ways, it was all very predictable. I bought myself a ticket to see Slipknot and traveled sixty miles to the concert. This was after Paul Gray, their founding bassist, had died of an accidental overdose, after they'd stopped setting one another on fire during their performances. Slipknot became popular in the late '90s, and they're still performing and making music twenty years later. It's still a big production. Contrary to the myths of my high school years, their masks are not taken from *The Nightmare Before Christmas*, and I suppose one good thing about being in a masked band is that aging is much less apparent. I only recognized half the songs, but I knew all the words to the familiar ones. I'd heard rumors about their drummer playing on a rotating platform that would eventually spin him upside-down, but they proved unfounded. At the end of the night, I caught one of the guitar picks thrown into the audience. I had turquoise hair at the time, and it was pouring rain when I left the auditorium. I rode home drenched and screaming with adrenaline. The next morning, the back of my neck looked bruised from where it'd taken on the color of my hair, but I went to work regardless.

Another time, I spent a few hours lying on the ground, baking in the May Atlanta heat, listening to the Deftones. This was at a day-long festival, and I was too tired to stand close to the stage or run through the mosh pit, but also unwilling to go home. I had reached the point of simultaneous thirst and needing to pee, yet it was worth it. I imagined the cover of their self-titled album: roses and a skull. Only the drums' vibrations in the earth kept me from feeling like I was floating away.

I said before I liked loud, fast music *as a teenager*, as if it's something I outgrew. This is misleading. I still routinely frighten unsuspecting passengers with the sound of booming double-time drums when I start my car's engine. I jump up and down until it feels like my neck is going to let my head fly right off my body. It's been a decade since I've hit a wall.

Flash forward to my weekly Thursday nights. The transition from fearful asceticism to racing the sun to sleep was boring, gradual, involved lots of therapy, and happened without my noticing. It seemed like one night I was afraid of what it would mean to see 3 a.m. too many times in a row, and then the next I was standing in my kitchen after dinner making coffee and grabbing a Red Bull out of the fridge.

How many times can we put on a costume until it is no longer a costume? On our way home from dancing, I think my friends and I are all a little in love. They have seen a sliver of the person I used to be, even if it is couched in dress-up and play-pretend. I feel exhausted and unburdened. I have been struck neither drunk nor manic. Nothing triggered, nothing spiraled; my fears unfounded. It feels like some kind of magic. Of course, I have not yet ascended beyond my resentments, and my taste in music hasn't much improved. But I am lucky to have survived growing up. The girl I once was and the woman I am now can both agree on this: Thankfully, there are no mirrors on the dance floor.

I drip sweat, my clothes heavy. When I hand Arizona a bunched up ten-dollar bill from my pocket for drinks, it is damp. I complain about my knees hurting, that I am *too old for this,* and then the next moment I am all hips. I alternate between Red Bull and water, and it's sometimes hard to tell what is the overenthusiastic bass and what is my heartbeat. The truth is I am always looking to forget myself. Even still.

It seems that no one on the dance floor thinks about anything—everyone is loose and spilling, swept up in currents of vodka and gin. I miss the feeling of not feeling.

But on those same nights, when I sit by myself on the sidelines and smoke cigarettes, my chest unhitches when the songs of my adolescence play. I return to my friends on the dance floor to soften, if only a little at a time, around the anger that moved through me when I was younger. I breathe deep and sing along.

So much of life and art is a matter of perspective and focus; to create a happy ending is often to look away at the right moment. Today I choose to linger here, no matter that it will not last. If I could freeze my friends mid-dance it would be in these quintessential poses: Mark, both his hands above his head, as if he is doing the wave; Arizona, her head cocked to the side, one foot in the air, a sandhill crane mid-flight; Felicity, perfect in miniature, looking away, elbows and knees angled in shapes of grace. We raise our voices, though still inaudible beneath the bass that sends the cheap plastic ashtrays scuttling across the stage, say that *we don't behave*, that we *believe in a thing called love*. Pause before the lights come up, before the sun rises in a few more hours.

flight

first hear it from a Flemish man. The information isn't relevant to the subject being discussed, and maybe that's why it sticks in my memory: Marx, misquoted. "It's often said that religion is the opium *for* the people." The Flemish man is the stereotype of a professor, favoring tweed jackets and wearing unkempt, graying curly hair. "But this is not the case."

Marx's actual quote reads: "Religion is the sigh of the oppressed creature, the heart of a heartless world, just as it is the spirit of spiritless conditions. It is the opium of the people."

I'm taking a course on intercultural communication in Brussels. Every Tuesday, I walk past perfect townhomes with windows that open sideways, past the sandwich shop, past the man who sells waffles embedded with beads of pearl sugar. The Flemish man teaches the class the correct way to ask for a private office should we ever be employed in the city. I write my first piece of creative nonfiction. It heavily features bus routes and fitted jeans. This is the season I fall back in with an ex-boyfriend.

Opium is made from the latex of a particular poppy and, like all opioids, reduces pain. Taken in inappropriate quantities, the consequences often exceed the original discomfort that prompted its usage. Speaking from personal experience, opium looks a lot like rabbit shit.

It is fall in Florida, and I am standing in the religion section of a Barnes & Noble. The air conditioning roars. The poppy at the center of my spine and the ouroboros at the nape of my neck are inky and stark above a low-backed pink shirt. I haven't been in this part of a bookstore since I worked in one during high school, but not much has changed. The Qurans are kept on the highest shelf, and the texts on the whole are overwhelmingly Christian—Bibles and angels and imagined post-rapture life. The book I am looking for takes its title from Habakkuk 3:19, *Hinds' Feet on High Places.*

I call Theresa at home, and she answers, Long Island in the mouth.

"I'm going to throw up standing here," I say. "No really, I think I'm gonna puke."

We stay on the phone till the book is in my hand. I hang up to stand in line to pay because I'm not a total monster. No one is in a hurry here. Moleskine notebooks and miniature bars of Godiva chocolate wink on display. The man behind me talks shit about my tattoos loud enough for me to hear him and suspect, but too quietly for me to confront him with confidence. I blame the shirt and how pink it is.

A few days later, Theresa eyes me over a cup of coffee so pale I suspect it is mostly creamer. Her bird bone fingers pick up a cigarette. Smoke washes the room foggy. The book I'd purchased lies on the table between us: paperback, white serif text on a purplish background. She says I'll read the first three chapters between now and next week when I'm to see her next. This is me trying to fix my life. This is her trying to help.

I want to believe in god. It seems important. Twelve-step programs claim to be nondenominational and nonreligious, but there is a strong undercurrent of Christianity.

I complain about the man in the bookstore, and Theresa shifts in her seat before redirecting the conversation. Do I remember the phone call? My overblown, metaphorical nausea? Had I heard myself?

"Alysia," she says, "you're prejudiced."

And I have nothing to say except that I'll read the chapters before I see her next.

I take a class with the heady title Religious Motifs of Doubt and Faith in Western Literature. This is at a private university with cobblestoned roads and silver minarets. The professor is somewhat of a mythic figure. His legend goes like this: He'd left the seminary to marry his wife, who had since died after many happy decades of marriage. Each year, he writes her a poem and reads it aloud at her grave on her birthday.

The class watches *Doubt*. Meryl Streep shudders beneath her black bonnet. I have just started to make friends, and her mannerisms in this film become something we'll return to. My friends are the ones who told me the story about our professor. We read Evelyn Waugh, Elie Wiesel, and E.L. Doctorow, and the only thing that seems certain after sixteen weeks is that these people will humor me (faith) in spite of myself (doubt).

I announce in class during a discussion, "I don't think we're meant to understand everything."

The professor nods. It feels like a blessing. I am always looking outside myself for a center.

For my final project, I write a short story about a junkie

kid who ODs and his friends try to mourn him, only to discover they're standing around the wrong unmarked grave. This story is true.

My teacher at the yoga studio is pale with long dark hair. She is a Pisces and a dancer and calls people *Babe* in a casual way that makes the person being addressed feel beautiful. A Ganesh tapestry hangs at the front of the room; an altar sits in the back corner, adorned with a small vase of fresh flowers, a brass Shiva, another wooden Ganesh. I've nearly kicked an idol more times than I can count.

She begins class playing the harmonium: "Om Gum Ganapatayei Namaha." But then we move and Curtis Mayfield trumpets "Move on Up" and Air purrs "Sexy Boy." The air conditioner does not work well. My teacher says *flight* as we raise our arms above our heads, palms pressing together; *flight* as we straighten our bent knees, becoming stars; *flight* as we spring forward from a crouch; *flight* as we try to lift our bodies skyward. I topple. In a yoga studio, I only ever feel perfect or wretched. I sit back on my heels and watch those around me, birds and angels alike, and try to think only loving, lovely thoughts.

My friend has more tattoos than anyone I've seen outside a tattoo shop. One day, when I am waxing on too much about ink and impermanence and bodies, they say, blunt, "Tattoos just look fucking cool."

They're right twice over. My first tattoo was that poppy in the middle of my back, which I got for no reason other than I wanted it. My most recent, my thirteenth, is another flower, a chrysanthemum blooming across my right triceps. It's all about the aesthetics. And my friend does look fucking cool. On their thigh is a red hammer and sickle next to a black ink portrait of Marx.

We are driving around Tampa listening to music. More accurately, they are driving and I am sitting in the passenger seat and chain-smoking. They let me do this even though they quit years ago. This is a thing we do in the summertime when the heat becomes too much. There's something about the velocity of a car that pairs well with loud music.

After his bit about opium, Marx goes on to write, "The overcoming of religion as the illusory happiness of the people is the demand for real happiness. The demand that they should abandon illusion about their condition is the *demand to give up conditions that require illusions.*"

He likes his italics. To look and see myself, to be unafraid and to work toward something more gentle and true—this is my test. I'll start small by admitting to the simple vanities I'd like to couch in mystery and meaning: Tattoos do look fucking cool.

The music is louder than usual tonight. The moon slivers through clouds and jasmine air snakes through the windows to press on our shoulders. Our friend has overdosed. We have just left her memorial. I barely cried. My test is ongoing. They turn up the volume even more and we sing.

I turn atheist while living in the Bible Belt. It isn't the ideal environment for the change. Most people in town have what they consider a *personal relationship* with Jesus. My kitchen is yellow, and I line the long windowsill above the sink with colored glass bottles. Everything about the room tries to hold in sunlight. My boyfriend is home rarely or all the time. He owns the house, and I prepare the meals. Saturday mornings, I wake before sunrise to make him sandwiches. I agreed to all this before I moved in.

Outside the house, I sit on the stoop and make phone calls and smoke cigarettes. I ring my best friend. Sometimes she talks to me and sometimes she talks to her children and sometimes I get it mixed up.

"I think I don't believe in god," I say.

"So you think you got yourself clean?" she asks.

We don't talk about it again.

I meet a woman who is more than twice my age and lives alone. She's been clean nearly thirty years, and when she says *Fuck* in public no one corrects her. She tells me she does not believe in any god or gods, capitalized or otherwise. Standing in my yellow kitchen, frying eggs I will never eat on an electric stovetop, I think of her often.

I stay at an ashram just south of Charlottesville, Virginia. We are surrounded by foothills. There is no meat or dairy or garlic or sugar in the cafeteria food, and I sign a piece of paper upon entry that says I will not consume any drugs or alcohol during my four-day stay, including nicotine. I keep a pack of cigarettes and a lighter in my glove box and nicotine gum in my duffel bag. It is hot outside. Everyone wears white and mostly long pants and sleeves. Before an afternoon meditation session, two women whisper loudly—it sounds more like two opossums chittering at dusk—about another whose shoulders are bare. A man has lines from the St. Francis prayer tattooed on his inner forearm: *Grant that I seek to comfort rather than to be comforted.*

I wake early for yoga classes, hike trails, sit in meditation three times a day, assist a monk writing letters to prisoners, and read *Man's Search for Meaning*. I am frantic. I check my body for ticks, stripping down in communal bathrooms, and worry I will become sick from the other practitioners. Two weeks earlier, my friend chose a medically induced coma hoping to get better and never woke up.

At the ashram, life's distractions are supposed to be stripped away. My brain ricochets. In yoga classes, we repeat poses to watch the body's changes—this time, the hips feel like this; the last time, they felt like that—learning to discern between injury and growth. Both are uncomfortable. The practice takes practice.

Outside, on the property, an interfaith temple sits in a dip of earth between hills. The building is shaped like a lotus and painted a gaudy blue and pink. I go to the second floor and sit cross-legged for a long time, crying. I mumble the same incantation I'd repeated to a friend some months earlier: *I can't, I can't, I can't.* With the right audience, it could be a prayer.

A monk tells me to be gentle with my mind. "It is so young," she says.

At night, after lights out, I drive off the property and smoke cigarettes. I hang my hand out the window like a teenager, trying to avoid the smoke sticking to my clothes. I chew Altoids afterward, and my mouth tastes rotten anyway.

My first time in a Buddhist meditation hall, I am the only person wearing jeans. The building is innocuous, tucked in among the businesses and cafes of sleepy Safety Harbor, Florida, and inside it seems like everyone knows better than me. The walls are white and clean, and I have no cash to leave for a donation. Row after row of cushioned chairs with linking metal frames face an altar. It is the focal point of the room. Food offerings and flowers surround a brass deity.

This type of meditation practice is sparse. Breathing in, breathing out. Listen. Focus. Notice the mind's inability to focus. I stay still because I am overcompensating. I sit barefoot, with my ankles crossed, and at the end, my feet feel like ants have taken up residence inside them. I open my eyes and see yellow and purple auras that linger despite fervent blinking. The halos are most noticeable against the white walls. I tell a resident about it.

"You stopped breathing," he says.

"I didn't," I insist.

"You weren't breathing *right*."

I am not expecting to be declared a mystic, but it turns out that even my breathing isn't good enough.

I read *Hallucinations* by Oliver Sacks while overseeing a middle-school detention room. I am partway through the chapter on hallucinogenic drugs and worry someone will ask about the book. We are in the middle of Indiana. Soybeans surround us. Police find a portable meth lab in the local Walmart bathroom. This is one kind of hell. In detention, students are only allowed to do schoolwork and to sit up straight. Putting their heads down or feet up, listening to music, eating, talking, drinking—none of these are permitted.

Instead of asking about the book, a student asks what the tattoo on my arm says. I do not answer. In later chapters, Sacks writes about seizures that precipitate religious conversions. People wake up believing in god; people wake up believing in nothing. Some parents at this school call the front office and do not know what grade their child is enrolled in. A colleague points out a student whose father stabbed his mother to death while he and his younger brother were in the house. Despite overseeing the detention room, I never sentence a single student to it, though I probably should. My tattoo is the last line of a short story by another writer: *And you, you ridiculous people, you expect me to help you.*

On the night Portugal wins the EuroCup, I smoke cigarettes in Lisbon with a poet who has blue eyes and a half-shaved head. My body feels like it is shimmering, maybe see-through. Everyone is outdoors. Men walk down the streets' centers, arms on one another's shoulders, singing. Car horns blare at bystanders waving the country's flag. The city is in love with itself and everyone in it. The poet smiles and teases, twangs of the Virginia hills in her voice.

"I double-dog dare you."

A day before, she'd lifted her body up into crow pose while wearing a dress and standing on a castle rampart. I'd egged her on. Peacocks screeched in the gardens below us. After she'd succeeded, it was my turn and I'd demurred.

Back on the street, she is just a little bit drunk and we are caught up in the night. "C'mon," she says.

"I've never done it before," I answer.

The sidewalk is slick and cobblestoned. I would like to be loved.

We are on a steep hill. I wait for a break in pedestrian traffic and hand the poet my cigarette. My hands plant on the smooth, dirty stones. I pitch my weight forward and my knees find a perch behind my shoulders. My center of gravity holds in my stomach. For a few seconds, I escape myself.

notes

Throughout the book, some names have been changed to protect individuals' privacy.

An Apology

1. Etymology is from the *Oxford English Dictionary*.
2. The Nirvana song in question is the ubiquitous "Smells Like Teen Spirit."
3. Cobain's interview was reprinted in the anthology *The Rolling Stone Interviews*, edited by Jann S. Wenner.
4. Lyrics are from Nirvana's "Heart-Shaped Box."
5. The terms "parallel universe," and "kindom of the sick and well" are taken from Susana Kaysen's *Girl, Interrupted* and Susan Sontag's *Illness as Metaphor*, respectively.
6. Notes about the song "All Apologies" come from Michael Azerrad's *Come as You Are: The Story of Nirvana*.

Wellness Index

1. There is an overabundance of information available about psychiatric medication. This essay is primarily based on my experience.
2. Lyrics are from Jefferson Airplane's "White Rabbit."
3. Salvador Dali included a girl jumping rope in a number of his paintings, as well as in his illustrations for *Alice in Wonderland*. He also sculpted the same girl in bronze—the piece shares its title with the book.
4. In the movie *Fear and Loathing in Las Vegas*, there is a scene in which Dr. Gonzo (played by Benicio del Toro) has eaten *a lot* of acid and sits clothed in a full bathtub, demanding to hear "White Rabbit."

Gutted

1. For more information about anorexia nervosa, including treatment, visit the National Eating Disorders Association website (nationaleatingdisorders.org), where they provide many resources and contact options.

Notes from the Cliff Face

1. More information on Old Rag can be found at the National Parks Services website at nps.gov/shen/planyourvisit/old-rag-hike-prep.htm.
2. The National Institute of Drug Abuse (drugabuse.gov) has many webpages dedicated to cocaine use as well as various drugs' affects on the brain.
3. The information about comorbidity comes from the American Psychiatric Association's *Diagnostic and Statistical Manual of Mental Disorders 5* (*DSM-5*) entry on bipolar disorder.
4. The unnamed story from Denis Johnson's *Jesus' Son* is "Car Crash While Hitchhiking."

Inheritance

1. The Susan Sontag quotes come from "In Plato's Cave" in her book *On Photography*.
2. Bipolar disorder information comes from the *DSM-5* and "The Role of the Family in the Course and Treatment of Bipolar Disorder," published in a 2007 issue of *Current Directions in Psychological Science*.
3. The Mary Karr quotes are taken from the chapter "The Truth Contract Twixt Writer and Reader" in *The Art of Memoir*.
4. The Eula Biss quote is taken from her essay "All Apologies" in *Notes from No Man's Land*.

Deep-Sea Creatures

1. The information about non-suicidal self injury comes from the *DSM-5's* entry on the subject.

Three Men

1. The 24-hour phone number for the National Suicide Prevention Lifeline is 1-800-273-8255.

Withdrawal

1. More information about bulimia, including treatment, can be found on the National Eating Disorders Association website, as previously listed.

Go Ask Alice

1. Bob Hicok's "Bottom of the Ocean" is from his collection *Insomnia Diary*.

2. For more on illness in the university, see Margaret Price's *Mad at School: Rhetorics of Mental Disability and Academic Life*.

3. The Michel Foucault quotes come from his book *Mental Illness and Psychology*.

4. The Lennard J. Davis quotes come from his introduction to the 4th edition of *The Disability Studies Reader*.

5. The mentioned study by Mark Zimmerman et al. is titled "Is Bipolar Disorder Overdiagnosed?" published in the *Journal of Clinical Psychiatry* 68(6).

Unsent

1. See David Ives' play "Sure Thing."

Indie Night at the Goth Club

1. The accompanying Spotify playlist for this essay is at burrowpress.com/goth

2. In order of appearance, the lyrics fragments referenced throughout this essay come from the following songs:
   - "Love Shack," The B-52s
   - "Under Pressure," Queen and David Bowie
   - "Wolf Like Me," TV on the Radio (text from the music video)
   - "Venus Fly," Grimes ft. Janelle Monáe
   - "Humble," Kendrick Lamar

- "Hotline Bling," Drake
- "Kill V. Maim," Grimes
- "I Believe in a Thing Called Love," The Darkness

3. The full text of Ben Ratliff's *New York Times* review "It's a Major Metal Band, and Even the Furniture Isn't Safe" is available online at nytimes.com/1998/06/22/arts/ pop-review-it-s-a-major- metal-band-and-even-the-furniture-isn-t-safe.html.

4. Though originally released on DVD, Tool's referenced music videos are now all available on YouTube.

Flight

1. This essay's shape was loosely inspired by Joan Didion's "Slouching Towards Bethlehem."

2. The quotes from Marx come from the introduction to his critique of Georg Hegel's *Elements of the Philosophy of Right*.

3. For more on the National Institute of Drug Abuse's classification of various opioids and their prevalence, see drugabuse.gov/drugs-abuse/opioids.

4. The Ganesh mantra can be loosely translated to "Om and salutations to the remover of obstacles."

acknowledgments

This book exists in the world as the result of so many tiny moments of impossible good fortune.

Thank you first to Ryan Rivas, Jared Silvia, Terry Godbey, and all the people at Burrow Press. I am so happy that this book has found its home with you. Thank you for being amazing editors and publishers and all-around excellent humans. You've built an amazing Florida literary community, and I'm so thankful to be part of the ~~secret illuminati cult~~ family. Moar fish!

Thank you to the editors, staff, and readers of the journals that have previously published (or are in the process of publishing) some of the essays from this collection: *Fourth Genre, St. Petersburg Review, Catapult, Gulf Coast,* and *LUMINA Online.*

Thank you to Ira for reading so many drafts of so many essays and so many emails. Your feedback and book recommendations have been formative and you probably should've gotten a course release for all the time you gifted me. Thank you for teaching me that the best way to know if an idea is a book is to write the damn thing. You have the most generous spirit, and I will always be down to go dumpling-hunting in whatever city we're in.

Thank you to Jill for introducing me to this little thing called creative nonfiction and for looking out for me along my journey. I cannot believe how I fell into your classroom by chance. Thank you for teaching me about resonance and about being unafraid. My life is infinitely brighter, kinder, and more brilliant because of you.

I have had so many excellent teachers throughout my life. Before this was a book, it was a thesis—thank you to Dinty and John for reading through this collection when it was a wee baby thing and for your insightful feedback. Thank you also to Heather, for so many lessons, but especially that of the three-legged cat; Erica, for teaching me the beauty and importance of a single sentence; Chanan, for telling me to write what it is that I want to write; and Parker, for the joys of a writing community.

I don't know where I'd be without all the writing groups and exchanges over the years. Thank you to all the good people of Disquiet as well as my MA and MFA cohorts. In particular, thank you to Alex, for keeping me writing during those early flailing drafts, and to Alison and Jubalee, for keeping me sane and surrounded by cats in the later ones. Sarah, thank you for the caffeine and the company. Thank you to Carmella for your energy and attention to detail, and thank you to Annalise for modeling how to do this damn writing thing and for being generally wonderful. Georgia, thank you for being the voice of balance and reason (that is, thank you for everything).

Thank you to the friends and medical professionals who allowed me to interview them during the process of writing these essays, and thank you to everyone who lived through this with me, both in the text and in the white spaces. Named in here or not, my life would not be the same without you. Special thanks to Alice; I love you with my whole cephalopod heart. Also thank you to Kat, Kelsey, and Brad for faithfully insisting that everything will be okay.

Finally, thank you to my parents for putting up with my shenanigans and for always encouraging my writing. My life has been filled with books and music and art, and I will always be grateful.

Photo © Eve Ettinger

about the author

Alysia Li Ying Sawchyn is a features editor for *The Rumpus* and currently lives in Northern Virginia. Her writing has appeared in *Fourth Genre, Brevity, Prairie Schooner*, and elsewhere. *A Fish Growing Lungs* is her first book.